This Journey Belongs To:

_____

NAME

_____

DATE

This workbook is not your ordinary workbook; it is a space where you can explore, grow, and learn new skills that empower you to strive toward your best self.

A
Life Changing
Workbook for
Boys Adulting

CHEYANNA MATTHIAS, MS

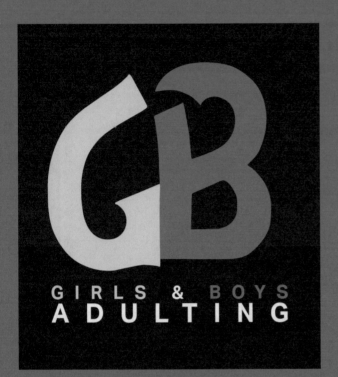

GIRLS & BOYS
ADULTING

Content

73   THE LOVE & CONNECTED BOY

93   THE CONFIDENT BOY

INTRODUCTION

Hey Bro! Welcome to your personal journey of growth and self-discovery! This workbook is more than just a collection of exercises, it's a tool designed to help you unlock your potential, explore new perspectives, and develop the skills you need to thrive in all areas of life.

Each page offers you the opportunity to reflect, create, and develop a mindset that will help you achieve your personal and professional goals. It is your space for personal development. Use it in a way that best supports your growth and goals. Make it your own, and let it be a tool to guide you on your path to success!

How to Use This Workbook

Set Aside Time:
Dedicate focused time to work through each section. Treat this workbook as a space for self-reflection and growth. You don't need to rush, take your time to fully engage with the exercises. A helpful tool to help guide you through the process and provide insight is: *A Quick Guide for Boys Adulting*.

Be Honest and Open:
The more authentic you are in your responses, the more you'll gain from this workbook. Reflect deeply on your thoughts, experiences, and challenges. There are no wrong answers, only opportunities to learn.

Take Notes:
Use the spaces provided to jot down your insights, thoughts, and reflections. Don't be afraid to write down extra thoughts or go beyond the prompts, this is your personal space.

Revisit and Reflect:
As you progress, take time to revisit earlier sections and reflect on how your thoughts and perspectives have evolved. Growth is a continuous process, and reviewing your progress will help reinforce your learning.

Apply What You Learn:
This workbook isn't just for thinking, it's for doing! Take the ideas, strategies, and insights you uncover and actively apply them in your daily life. Whether it's through goal setting, mindset shifts, or new habits. Turn these lessons into actions!

Seek Support:
If you find certain exercises difficult or thought-provoking, consider discussing your responses with a friend, mentor, coach, or counselor. Sometimes, talking through your thoughts can lead to even deeper understanding. Follow Girls & Boys Adulting @gbadulting for additional support.

Enjoy the Journey:
This workbook is a journey toward becoming your best self. Enjoy the process, and remember that personal growth is about progress, not perfection. Celebrate your insights and breakthroughs along the way!

I am resilient enough to make it through hard times!

THE
BASIC
BOY

As important as our basic needs are, sometimes they are the first things to be neglected in times of hardship or stress. Step into this section to gain tools for evaluating, understanding, and obtaining your basic needs.

NEEDS ASSESSMENT

Let's see where you fall on the "Adulting" scale. This worksheet will help you gauge what aspects of your life are important to you right now, or need to focus on. **Directions**: Answer each question associated with the category, then rank each category by its importance to you, 1 being a *low level need* and 5 being a *high level need*.

FOOD

1. Do you have access to enough food daily?
   ☐ Yes   ☐ No

2. Do you have access to nutritious food?
   ☐ Yes   ☐ No

1	2	3	4	5

1 = Low Level Need   High Level Need = 5

WATER

3. Do you have access to clean water daily?
   ☐ Yes   ☐ No

4. Do you intake water daily?
   ☐ Yes   ☐ No

1	2	3	4	5

1 = Low Level Need   High Level Need = 5

SHELTER

5. Do you have stable and secure housing?
   ☐ Yes   ☐ No

6. Do you have good living conditions
   (e.g., safety, hygienic, occupancy)?
   ☐ Yes   ☐ No

1	2	3	4	5

1 = Low Level Need   High Level Need = 5

SLEEP

7. Are you getting enough sleep each night?
   ☐ Yes   ☐ No

8. Do you wake up feeling well rested?
   ☐ Yes   ☐ No

1	2	3	4	5

1 = Low Level Need   High Level Need = 5

The Basic Boy

NEEDS ASSESSMENT

FINANCES

9. Do you have a stable income?
   ☐ Yes   ☐ No

10. Are you able to pay all of your expenses?
    ☐ Yes   ☐ No

11. Are you able to save and invest money?
    ☐ Yes   ☐ No

1	2	3	4	5

1 = Low Level Need   High Level Need = 5

HEALTH

12. Are you treating or have treated all of your health issues?
    ☐ Yes   ☐ No

13. Do you have access to healthcare services and insurance?
    ☐ Yes   ☐ No

1	2	3	4	5

1 = Low Level Need   High Level Need = 5

SAFETY

14. Do you feel safe in your current living environment?
    ☐ Yes   ☐ No

15. Are you addressing or have addressed immediate threats to your physical safety?
    ☐ Yes   ☐ No

1	2	3	4	5

1 = Low Level Need   High Level Need = 5

The Safe & Secured Boy

NEEDS ASSESSMENT

SOCIAL

16. Do you feel connected and supported?
    ☐ Yes   ☐ No

17. Do you interact with others regularly?
    ☐ Yes   ☐ No

1	2	3	4	5

1 = Low Level Need   High Level Need = 5

FAMILY

18. Do you interact with your family?
    ☐ Yes   ☐ No

19. Do you have supportive family relationships?
    ☐ Yes   ☐ No

1	2	3	4	5

1 = Low Level Need   High Level Need = 5

FRIENDS

20. Do you interact with friends?
    ☐ Yes   ☐ No

21. Do you have supportive friend relationships?
    ☐ Yes   ☐ No

1	2	3	4	5

1 = Low Level Need   High Level Need = 5

COMMUNITY

22. Do you have a community that you belong to?
    ☐ Yes   ☐ No

23. Are you involved in community groups or organizations?
    ☐ Yes   ☐ No

1	2	3	4	5

1 = Low Level Need   High Level Need = 5

The Loved & Connected Boy

WWW.GBADULTING.ORG

NEEDS ASSESSMENT

ESTEEM	24. Do you feel confident and capable in your daily activities? ☐ Yes ☐ No 25. Are you setting and achieving personal goals? ☐ Yes ☐ No	**1** **2** **3** **4** **5** 1 = Low Level Need High Level Need = 5
STATUS	26. Are you satisfied with where you are in your social life? ☐ Yes ☐ No 27. Are you satisfied with where you are in your professional life? ☐ Yes ☐ No	**1** **2** **3** **4** **5** 1 = Low Level Need High Level Need = 5
RECOGNITION	28. Do you receive recognition for your achievements at work, school, or in your community? ☐ Yes ☐ No 29. Are you involved in activities that help you feel valued and respected? ☐ Yes ☐ No	**1** **2** **3** **4** **5** 1 = Low Level Need High Level Need = 5

The Confident Boy

NEEDS ASSESSMENT

PURPOSE

30. Do you feel a sense of purpose in your daily life?
    ☐ Yes   ☐ No
31. Are you working on long-term goals that are meaningful to you?
    ☐ Yes   ☐ No

1	2	3	4	5

1 = Low Level Need   High Level Need = 5

AUTHENCITY

32. Do you express your genuine thoughts and feelings, even if they are different from those around you?
    ☐ Yes   ☐ No
33. Do you feel you can be your true self in most situations?
    ☐ Yes   ☐ No

1	2	3	4	5

1 = Low Level Need   High Level Need = 5

CREATIVITY

34. Are you spontaneous?
    ☐ Yes   ☐ No

35. Do you pursue hobbies and projects?
    ☐ Yes   ☐ No

1	2	3	4	5

1 = Low Level Need   High Level Need = 5

DEVELOPMENT

36. Are you engaged in activities that help you grow professionally and personally?
    ☐ Yes   ☐ No

37. Do you have opportunities to pursue your passions and interests?
    ☐ Yes   ☐ No

1	2	3	4	5

1 = Low Level Need   High Level Need = 5

The Purposefully Driven Boy

WWW.GBADULTING.ORG

NEEDS ASSESSMENT

Directions: Take this time to reflect on all of the questions, and the areas that you ranked as high level needs. Remember all areas of need are important. Commend yourself for any questions you were able to answer yes to. Questions you were unsure of or answered no to, these are your developing areas and indicate your current needs. Put a check mark in the box of your identified needs. These would be the areas you rated a 4 or above, which should be areas that are associated with the questions where you answered no.

Food
THE BASIC BOY
☐

Water
THE BASIC BOY
☐

Shelter
THE BASIC BOY
☐

Sleep
THE BASIC BOY
☐

Finances
THE SAFE & SECURED BOY
☐

Health
THE SAFE & SECURED BOY
☐

Safety
THE SAFE & SECURED BOY
☐

Social
THE LOVED & CONNECTED BOY
☐

Family
THE LOVED & CONNECTED BOY
☐

Friends
THE LOVED & CONNECTED BOY
☐

Community
THE LOVED & CONNECTED BOY
☐

Esteem
THE CONFIDENT BOY
☐

Status
THE CONFIDENT BOY
☐

Recognition
THE CONFIDENT BOY
☐

Purpose
THE PURPOSEFULLY DRIVEN BOY
☐

Authenticity
THE PURPOSEFULLY DRIVEN BOY
☐

Creativity
THE PURPOSEFULLY DRIVEN BOY
☐

Development
THE PURPOSEFULLY DRIVEN BOY
☐

NEEDS ASSESSMENT

Directions: Circle all of the areas of need that you checked off on the previous page. Then write down your top 9 areas of need. After you have figured out your current needs, you are now going to determine your top 3 areas of focus by the Chapter. For instance, if you ranked *Food* as a *high level need or a 4*, then you would circle *"The Basic Boy"*.

AREAS OF NEED

Food   Water   Shelter   Sleep   Finances

Health   Safety   Social   Family

Friends   Community   Esteem   Status   Recognition

Purpose   Authenticity   Creativity   Development

TOP 9 AREAS OF NEED

1. _____
2. _____
3. _____
4. _____
5. _____
6. _____
7. _____
8. _____
9. _____

TOP 3 AREAS OF FOCUS

The Basic Boy

The Safe & Secured Boy

The Loved & Connected Boy

The Confident Boy

The Purposefully Driven Boy

REFLECTION POINT: NEEDS

Exercise: Make sure you are in a comfortable space, free of distractions. Close your eyes, and visualize yourself meeting all of your needs. What does that look like for you? Think of the reasons why it is not a reality for you right now and the steps you need to take to make it a reality, and write your thoughts down. Be honest and detailed with your response.

If I can visualize it, then I can obtain it!

WEEKLY BASIC NEEDS PLAN

Directions: Use this planner to plan out a week's worth of needs. Think about how and where you are going to get your needs met.

	Food	Sleep	Breathe
Monday	MEAL 1: _____ MEAL 2: _____ MEAL 3: _____	HOURS: ____ SLEEP BY: ____ AWAKE BY: ____	EXERCISE _____ _____ _____
Tuesday	MEAL 1: _____ MEAL 2: _____ MEAL 3: _____	HOURS: ____ SLEEP BY: ____ AWAKE BY: ____	EXERCISE _____ _____ _____
Wednesday	MEAL 1: _____ MEAL 2: _____ MEAL 3: _____	HOURS: ____ SLEEP BY: ____ AWAKE BY: ____	EXERCISE _____ _____ _____
Thursday	MEAL 1: _____ MEAL 2: _____ MEAL 3: _____	HOURS: ____ SLEEP BY: ____ AWAKE BY: ____	EXERCISE _____ _____ _____
Friday	MEAL 1: _____ MEAL 2: _____ MEAL 3: _____	HOURS: ____ SLEEP BY: ____ AWAKE BY: ____	EXERCISE _____ _____ _____
Saturday	MEAL 1: _____ MEAL 2: _____ MEAL 3: _____	HOURS: ____ SLEEP BY: ____ AWAKE BY: ____	EXERCISE _____ _____ _____
Sunday	MEAL 1: _____ MEAL 2: _____ MEAL 3: _____	HOURS: ____ SLEEP BY: ____ AWAKE BY: ____	EXERCISE _____ _____ _____

I am proud of my journey!

SMART Goals

Explore your long and short term goals. Understand your experiences and how they can affect the goal planning and setting process. Make goals that are *specific*, *measurable*, *achievable*, *relevant*, **and** *time-bound*.

Specific
Measurable
Achievable
Relevant
Time-bound

Specific Make goals clear Ex: "I will ~~get fit~~ run...	
Measurable Make goals trackable Ex: ...~~more often~~ once a week...	
Achievable Make goals realistic Ex: ...for at least ~~10~~ 1 mile...	
Relevant Make goals about you Ex: ...so I can join a run club...	
Time-bound Give yourself a deadline Ex: ...~~one day~~ by the end of 2024.	

I am achieving my goals!

GOAL PLANNING TRACKER

Area of Focus
- ☐ The Basic Boy
- ☐ The Safe & Secured Boy
- ☐ The Loved & Connected Boy
- ☐ The Confident Boy
- ☐ The Purposefully Driven Boy

Area of Focus
- ☐ Food
- ☐ Water
- ☐ Shelter
- ☐ Sleep
- ☐ Finances
- ☐ Authenticity
- ☐ Health
- ☐ Safety
- ☐ Social
- ☐ Family
- ☐ Friends
- ☐ Creativity
- ☐ Community
- ☐ Esteem
- ☐ Status
- ☐ Recognition
- ☐ Purpose
- ☐ Development

Long-Term Goal 1

How **important** is it that you make this change? ⓪①②③④⑤⑥⑦⑧⑨⑩
Not at all ... Very

Short-Term Goal 1

How **confident** are you that you are able to make this change? ⓪①②③④⑤⑥⑦⑧⑨⑩
Not at all ... Very

How **important** is it that you make this change? ⓪①②③④⑤⑥⑦⑧⑨⑩
Not at all ... Very

I REACHED MY GOAL THIS WEEK! 1 ☐ 2 ☐ 3 ☐ 4 ☐ 5 ☐ 6 ☐ 7 ☐ 8 ☐

Short-Term Goal 2

How **confident** are you that you are able to make this change? ⓪①②③④⑤⑥⑦⑧⑨⑩
Not at all ... Very

How **important** is it that you make this change? ⓪①②③④⑤⑥⑦⑧⑨⑩
Not at all ... Very

I REACHED MY GOAL THIS WEEK! 1 ☐ 2 ☐ 3 ☐ 4 ☐ 5 ☐ 6 ☐ 7 ☐ 8 ☐

Short-Term Goal 3

How **confident** are you that you are able to make this change? ⓪①②③④⑤⑥⑦⑧⑨⑩
Not at all ... Very

How **important** is it that you make this change? ⓪①②③④⑤⑥⑦⑧⑨⑩
Not at all ... Very

I REACHED MY GOAL THIS WEEK! 1 ☐ 2 ☐ 3 ☐ 4 ☐ 5 ☐ 6 ☐ 7 ☐ 8 ☐

I attract success!

GOAL PLANNING TRACKER

Area of Focus	**Area of Focus**		
☐ The Basic Boy	☐ Food	☐ Health	☐ Community
☐ The Safe & Secured Boy	☐ Water	☐ Safety	☐ Esteem
☐ The Loved & Connected Boy	☐ Shelter	☐ Social	☐ Status
☐ The Confident Boy	☐ Sleep	☐ Family	☐ Recognition
☐ The Purposefully Driven Boy	☐ Finances	☐ Friends	☐ Purpose
	☐ Authenticity	☐ Creativity	☐ Development

Long-Term Goal 2

How **important** is it that you make this change? ⓪ ① ② ③ ④ ⑤ ⑥ ⑦ ⑧ ⑨ ⑩
Not at all   Very

Short-Term Goal 1

How **confident** are you that you are able to make this change? ⓪ ① ② ③ ④ ⑤ ⑥ ⑦ ⑧ ⑨ ⑩
Not at all   Very

How **important** is it that you make this change? ⓪ ① ② ③ ④ ⑤ ⑥ ⑦ ⑧ ⑨ ⑩
Not at all   Very

I REACHED MY GOAL THIS WEEK!   1 ☐   2 ☐   3 ☐   4 ☐   5 ☐   6 ☐   7 ☐   8 ☐

Short-Term Goal 2

How **confident** are you that you are able to make this change? ⓪ ① ② ③ ④ ⑤ ⑥ ⑦ ⑧ ⑨ ⑩
Not at all   Very

How **important** is it that you make this change? ⓪ ① ② ③ ④ ⑤ ⑥ ⑦ ⑧ ⑨ ⑩
Not at all   Very

I REACHED MY GOAL THIS WEEK!   1 ☐   2 ☐   3 ☐   4 ☐   5 ☐   6 ☐   7 ☐   8 ☐

Short-Term Goal 3

How **confident** are you that you are able to make this change? ⓪ ① ② ③ ④ ⑤ ⑥ ⑦ ⑧ ⑨ ⑩
Not at all   Very

How **important** is it that you make this change? ⓪ ① ② ③ ④ ⑤ ⑥ ⑦ ⑧ ⑨ ⑩
Not at all   Very

I REACHED MY GOAL THIS WEEK!   1 ☐   2 ☐   3 ☐   4 ☐   5 ☐   6 ☐   7 ☐   8 ☐

I am motivated, persistent, and successful!

GOAL PLANNING TRACKER

Area of Focus
☐ The Basic Boy
☐ The Safe & Secured Boy
☐ The Loved & Connected Boy
☐ The Confident Boy
☐ The Purposefully Driven Boy

Area of Focus

☐ Food	☐ Health	☐ Community
☐ Water	☐ Safety	☐ Esteem
☐ Shelter	☐ Social	☐ Status
☐ Sleep	☐ Family	☐ Recognition
☐ Finances	☐ Friends	☐ Purpose
☐ Authenticity	☐ Creativity	☐ Development

Long-Term Goal 3

How **important** is it that you make this change?   ⓪ ① ② ③ ④ ⑤ ⑥ ⑦ ⑧ ⑨ ⑩
Not at all   Very

Short-Term Goal 1

How **confident** are you that you are able to make this change?   ⓪ ① ② ③ ④ ⑤ ⑥ ⑦ ⑧ ⑨ ⑩
Not at all   Very

How **important** is it that you make this change?   ⓪ ① ② ③ ④ ⑤ ⑥ ⑦ ⑧ ⑨ ⑩
Not at all   Very

I REACHED MY GOAL THIS WEEK!   1 2 3 4 5 6 7 8
☐ ☐ ☐ ☐ ☐ ☐ ☐ ☐

Short-Term Goal 2

How **confident** are you that you are able to make this change?   ⓪ ① ② ③ ④ ⑤ ⑥ ⑦ ⑧ ⑨ ⑩
Not at all   Very

How **important** is it that you make this change?   ⓪ ① ② ③ ④ ⑤ ⑥ ⑦ ⑧ ⑨ ⑩
Not at all   Very

I REACHED MY GOAL THIS WEEK!   1 2 3 4 5 6 7 8
☐ ☐ ☐ ☐ ☐ ☐ ☐ ☐

Short-Term Goal 3

How **confident** are you that you are able to make this change?   ⓪ ① ② ③ ④ ⑤ ⑥ ⑦ ⑧ ⑨ ⑩
Not at all   Very

How **important** is it that you make this change?   ⓪ ① ② ③ ④ ⑤ ⑥ ⑦ ⑧ ⑨ ⑩
Not at all   Very

I REACHED MY GOAL THIS WEEK!   1 2 3 4 5 6 7 8
☐ ☐ ☐ ☐ ☐ ☐ ☐ ☐

I am worthy of success!

MINDFULNESS ACTIVITIES

Mindfulness is a practice of paying attention to the present moment without trying to change it or judge it. While being in the moment, you are called to observe your thoughts, feelings, and sensations. **Directions**: Pick one of the activities below, and complete one.

FIVE SENSES

Pay attention to each of your senses, one after the other using this criteria:

- **5** things you **see**
- **4** things you **feel**
- **3** things you **hear**
- **2** things you **smell**
- **1** thing you **taste**

BODY SCAN

Pay close attention to the sensations throughout your body. Start with your feet, and move upwards through your legs, groin, abdomen, chest, back, shoulders, arms, hands, neck, and face. Spend 15 seconds to 1 minute on each body part.

MINDFUL WALK

While walking, notice how your body moves and feels with each step. Expand your awareness to your surroundings. What do you feel, see, hear, and smell? You can do this exercise during daily activities.

MINDFULNESS MEDITATION

Sit or lay in a comfortable place, and begin paying attention to your breathing. Notice the physical sensation of air filling your lungs, and then slowly leaving. When your mind wanders, acknowledge your thoughts and turn your attention back to breathing.

As I let go, I feel myself thriving in all areas of my life!

WATER INTAKE DIAGRAM

Drinking enough water every day is important for good health. Our bodies rely on it for many of its functions. Water helps protect our body organs and tissue, get rid of waste, lubricates joints, and supports the growth and reproduction of cells.

WATER NEEDS CALCULATOR

Your Body Weight = oz
2

WATER NEEDS CALCULATED

150lbs = 75 oz
2

HYDRATING FOODS

Watermelon
Strawberries
Tomatoes
Celery
Spinach
Mangoes
Blueberries
Cantaloupes
Honeydew Melons
Broccoli
Peaches
Oranges
Pineapples
Bell Pepers
Cucumbers
Lettuce
Squash
Zucchini
Cabbage
Cauliflower

DEHYDRATION SIGNS

Dizziness
Dark Urine
Thirst
Dry Mouth
Headache
Fatigue

WATER INTAKE TRACKER

Directions: Each glass represents 8oz. Shade in the amount of water you drank each day.

1
2
3
4
5
6
7
8
9
10
11
12
13
14
15
16

17
18
19
20
21
22
23
24
25
26
27
28
29
30
31

MONTH:

ACTIVITY LIST

Visit a park	Try a new food	Visit a museum
Play cards	Go swimming	Write in a journal
See the sunrise/sunset	Call a friend	Read a book
Exercise	Bake a dessert	Go to a concert
Listen to music	Volunteer	Go for a bike ride
Visit a friend	Plan a vacation	Draw/Paint/Color
Explore a new place	Take pictures	Cook a meal
Meditate	Go for a walk	Learn a language
Work in a garden	Watch a movie	Have a picnic

DAILY ROUTINE

Directions: Create a schedule of activities that will lead to you having positive experiences in your day. If you are feeling unmotivated, it might be difficult to complete large or complex tasks. If this is the case, start with simple goals and gradually add more challenging activities.

DAY	MORNING	AFTERNOON	EVENING
Example	*Wake up by 9 am* *Go for a morning walk*	*Eat a hearty lunch*	*Learn a language* *Read a book*
Monday			
Tuesday			
Wednesday			
Thursday			
Friday			
Saturday			
Sunday			

I am making the life I want!

MY PLATE DIAGRAM

Use this as a guide for creating healthy, balanced meals. You can choose to eat them on the go, when you go out to eat, packed in a lunch box, or at the table.

Protein (20-25%)

Carbohydrates (10-20%)

Fruits & Vegetables (60-70%)

GROCERTY LIST GAME PLAN

To create the healthiest plate, keep these food items in mind to help you navigate the grocery store.

FRUITS

Banana
Grape
Raspberry
Papaya
Passion Fruit
Date
Blackberry
Plum
Watermelon
Strawberry
Tomato
Mango
Blueberry
Cantaloupe
Honeydew Melon
Peach
Orange
Pineapple
Apple
Pear
Avocado
Grapefruit
Kiwi
Cherry
Pomegranate
Apricot

VEGETABLES

Celery
Spinach
Broccoli
Bell Pepper
Cucumber
Lettuce
Squash
Zucchini
Cabbage
Cauliflower
Kale
Green Peas
Beets
Carrot
Brussel Sprout
Onion
Asparagus
Seaweed
Alfalfa Sprout
Bok Choy
Red Cabbage
Garlic
Swiss Chard
Green Banana
Mushroom
Parsley

PROTEIN

Egg
Nuts
Ground Bison
Lentils
Pork Tenderloin
Tuna
Cottage Cheese
Peanut Butter
Chicken Breast
Scallops
Edamame
Lean Beef
Salmon
Tilapia
Tofu
Greek Yogurt
Tempeh
Almond Butter
Chia Seeds
Soy
Tilapia
Turkey Breast
Ground Lamb
Chickpeas
Black Beans
Shrimp

CARBOHYDRATES

Oats
Brown Rice
Sweet Potato
White Potato
Quinoa
Kidney Beans

Multigrain Cereal
Whole Wheat Pasta
Whole Wheat Bread
Pumpkin
Whole Wheat Tortilla
Corn

STICK TO WHOLE FOODS AND AVOID PACKAGED/PREPARED FOODS.

SLEEP HYGIENE

Sleep is an essential part of maintaining good physical and mental health. Good sleep can help restore your body's energy levels, regulate your emotions, and process and organize memories. Poor sleep can cause your memory to be impaired, slow down your brain functioning, increase your stress levels, increase your blood pressure, and exacerbate mental health problems. It can lead to mood swings, anxiety, irritability, and depression. Sleep is important! Use these tips and this checklist to improve your sleep.

TIPS

- Set a schedule
- Avoid caffeine later in the day
- Avoid napping
- Use your bed only for sleep & sex
- Make your bedroom comfortable
- Don't force yourself to sleep
- Eat fruits & vegetables

CHECKLIST

☐ **Get up at the same time every day**

☐ **Sleep at least 7 to 9 consecutive hours**

☐ **Get out of bed immediately after waking up**

☐ **Get exposure to bright light**

☐ **Exercise regularly**

☐ **Avoid excessive liquids in the evening**

☐ **Unplug an hour before bed**

☐ **Get up & try again.** If you have not been able to fall asleep after 20 minutes, get up and do something calming or boring until you feel tired, then return to bed and try again. Sit quietly in a chair with the lights off, or read something boring. Avoid doing anything stimulating.

SLEEP DIARY

Directions: Use this diary to keep track of your sleep patterns. Track your caffeine intake by noting the amount of drinks and the times of day you tend to have caffeine (*morning (M), afternoon (A), evening (E)*).

		DAY 1	DAY 2	DAY 3	DAY 4	DAY 5	DAY 6	DAY 7
MORNING CHECK-IN	WEEK DAY							
	BED TIME	AM PM	AM PM	AM PM	AM PM	AM PM	AM PM	AM PM
	AWAKE TIME	AM PM	AM PM	AM PM	AM PM	AM PM	AM PM	AM PM
	ASLEEP TIME	Hrs	Hrs	Hrs	Hrs	Hrs	Hrs	Hrs
	WAIT TIME	Mins	Mins	Mins	Mins	Mins	Mins	Mins
	SLEEP ISSUES							
	SLEEP QUALITY							
	I FEEL							
	WOKE UP	Times	Times	Times	Times	Times	Times	Times
EVENING CHECK-IN	TOOK A NAP?							
	CAFFEINE	#	#	#	#	#	#	#
	CAFFEINE TIME	M A E	M A E	M A E	M A E	M A E	M A E	M A E
	EXERCISE	Mins Hrs	Mins Hrs	Mins Hrs	Mins Hrs	Mins Hrs	Mins Hrs	Mins Hrs
	DROWSY?							
	MOOD							
	BEDTIME ACTIVITY							

I succeed and thrive when I feel rested and fulfilled!

HOUSING ASSESSMENT

This tool can be used to determine whether your housing is sufficient for you.

CURRENT LIVING SITUATION

- [ ] With a family member (does not pay rent)
- [ ] With a friend (does not pay rent)
- [ ] With a host family (does not pay rent)
- [ ] Independently living alone (pays rent)
- [ ] Independently living with friends/roommates (pays rent)
- [ ] Independently living with family (pays rent)
- [ ] Subsidized housing program (program pays rent)

- [ ] Owns home
- [ ] Human trafficking shelter
- [ ] Homeless Shelter
- [ ] Domestic violence shelter
- [ ] Street/Homeless/Couch surfing
- [ ] Other: _____
_____

Feelings about your current living situation. (select all that apply)
- [ ] Safe
- [ ] Unsafe
- [ ] Scared
- [ ] Isolated
- [ ] Happy
- [ ] Neutral
- [ ] Other: _____

Do you want to stay in your current living situation long term?
- [ ] Yes
- [ ] No
- [ ] Unsure

HOUSING PREFERENCES

What is your ideal living situation? _____
_____
_____

What is your desired housing location? (e.g., near work, a specific neighborhood, or public transportation accessibility) _____
_____
_____

I am deserving of a safe place to call home!

WWW.GBADULTING.ORG

GOAL CHECKPOINT

Keeping track of your goals is an important step in accomplishing your goals. **Directions**: Reflect on the goals you have created for yourself. Think of the obstacles you are facing or have faced while trying to reach your goal, and possible changes you need to make.

Long-Term Goal 1

Target Date	I REACHED MY GOAL	Still Relevant?	Still Achievable?
_____	☐	☐ Yes ☐ No	☐ Yes ☐ No

Obstacles to reaching your goal:

1. _____
2. _____
3. _____
4. _____
5. _____

Strengths that will help you achieve your goal:

1. _____
2. _____
3. _____
4. _____
5. _____

How do you plan to respond to each obstacle: _____
_____
_____
_____

Things you will need to do to achieve your goal: _____
_____
_____
_____

What can you do tomorrow to work toward your goal: _____
_____
_____
_____

GOAL CHECKPOINT

Long-Term Goal 2 _____

Target Date	I REACHED MY GOAL	Still Relevant?	Still Achievable?
_____	☐	☐ Yes ☐ No	☐ Yes ☐ No

Obstacles to reaching your goal:

1. _____
2. _____
3. _____
4. _____
5. _____

Strengths that will help you achieve your goal:

1. _____
2. _____
3. _____
4. _____
5. _____

How do you plan to respond to each obstacle: _____

_____

_____

_____

Things you will need to do to achieve your goal: _____

_____

_____

_____

What can you do tomorrow to work toward your goal: _____

_____

_____

_____

I overcome challenges and obstacles!

GOAL CHECKPOINT

Long-Term Goal 3

Target Date   **I REACHED MY GOAL** ☐   **Still Relevant?** ☐ Yes ☐ No   **Still Achievable?** ☐ Yes ☐ No

_____

Obstacles to reaching your goal:
1. _____
2. _____
3. _____
4. _____
5. _____

Strengths that will help you achieve your goal:
1. _____
2. _____
3. _____
4. _____
5. _____

How do you plan to respond to each obstacle: _____

_____

_____

_____

Things you will need to do to achieve your goal: _____

_____

_____

_____

What can you do tomorrow to work toward your goal: _____

_____

_____

_____

I can create the life I want to live!

I deserve to move through life with ease!

THE SAFE & SECURED BOY

Having your basic needs met is one thing, but ensuring that you are able to maintain them is another thing. Take a deep dive into this next section to utilize tools that will help you obtain the security you are looking for in life.

MY ACE SCORE

> **Trigger Alert!** Adverse Childhood Experiences (ACEs) refers to potentially traumatic experiences that occurred in early life. This quiz will help raise awareness about the potential impact of ACEs on your life. Higher ACEs are often associated with challenges to life, including high risk of health problems. Though this assessment has limitations*, it can be a great tool for learning how to build resiliency. **Directions**: For each "yes" answer, add 1. The total number at the end is your cumulative number of ACEs.

Before your 18th birthday:

1. Did a parent or other adult in the household often or very often...
   a. Swear at you, insult you, put you down, or humiliate you?
   b. Act in a way that made you afraid that you might be physically hurt?

   ☐ Yes   ☐ No

2. Did a parent or other adult in the household often or very often...
   a. Push, grab, slap, or throw something at you? or
   b. Ever hit you so hard that you had marks or were injured?

   ☐ Yes   ☐ No

3. Did an adult or person at least 5 years older than you ever...
   a. Touch or fondle you, or have you touch their body in a sexual way? or
   b. Attempt or actually have oral, anal, or vaginal intercourse with you?

   ☐ Yes   ☐ No

4. Did you often or very often feel that...
   a. No one in your family loved you, or thought you were important or special? or
   b. Your family didn't look out for each other, feel close to each other, or support each other?

   ☐ Yes   ☐ No

5. Did you often or very often feel that...
   a. You didn't have enough to eat, had to wear dirty clothes, and had no one to protect you? or
   b. Your parents were too drunk or high to take care of you or take you to the doctor if you needed it?

   ☐ Yes   ☐ No

MY ACE SCORE

6. Were your parents ever separated or divorced?

☐ Yes ☐ No

7. Was your parent or caregiver:
   a. Often or very often pushed, grabbed, slapped, or had something thrown at him/her? or
   b. Sometimes, often, or very often kicked, bitten, hit with a fist, or hit with something hard? or
   c. Ever repeatedly hit, over at least a few minutes, or threatened with a gun or knife?

☐ Yes ☐ No

8. Did you live with anyone who was a problem drinker or alcoholic, or who used street drugs?

☐ Yes ☐ No

9. Was a household member depressed or mentally ill, or did a household member attempt suicide?

☐ Yes ☐ No

10. Did a household member go to prison?

☐ Yes ☐ No

My ACE Score: _____ **/10**

Limitations*

- **Individual differences** - not all children who experience multiple ACEs will have poor outcomes and not all children who experience no ACEs will avoid poor outcomes. A high ACEs score is just an indicator of greater risk
- **Stressors outside the household** - violence, chaotic environment, poverty, lack of services, racism, other forms of discrimination, or isolation
- **Protective factors** - supportive relationships, community services, or skill-building activities

Everyone is capable of healing!

STRESS MANAGEMENT

Stress is an emotional and physical response to demanding situations. It is the way your body responds to the day-to-day struggles and demands of life. A little bit of stress can be healthy, and keep you alert and productive. **Directions**: Put a checkmark next to or write in your biggest stressors in each category.

DAILY HASSLES (COMMON ANNOYANCES IN DAILY LIFE)

- ☐ Limited free time
- ☐ Work problems
- ☐ Lack of sleep
- ☐ Homework
- ☐ Chores
- ☐ Traffic
- ☐ Arguments
- ☐ Dating

_____

_____

MAJOR LIFE CHANGES (IMPORTANT EVENTS THAT REQUIRE ADJUSTMENT)

- ☐ Moving
- ☐ Major illness/injury
- ☐ Divorce
- ☐ Birth of a child
- ☐ New job
- ☐ New school
- ☐ Death of someone
- ☐ New relationship

_____

_____

LIFE CIRCUMSTANCES (PERMANENT OR LONG-TERM, THAT MAKE LIFE MORE DIFFICULT)

- ☐ Job dissatisfaction
- ☐ Discrimination
- ☐ Unsafe living
- ☐ Financial problems
- ☐ Disability
- ☐ Chronic illness
- ☐ Conflicting values
- ☐ Relationship issues

_____

_____

REFLECTION POINT: STRESS

Exercise: Make sure you are in a comfortable space, free of distractions. Describe your largest source of stress here. Think about why it is your largest source of stress, and how it has gotten to be that way. You can add one or two more stressors that you are experiencing. Then write down any habits or tendencies you have that worsen the situation when faced with unpleasant emotions. Be honest and detailed.

I am stronger than my stress!

STRESS MANAGEMENT

Not all stress is bad. The stress response is a powerful tool used by your body to increase the odds of overcoming obstacles. When you experience stress intensely or it lasts for a long time, it can result in serious physical, emotional, and behavioral symptoms. Many people take shortcuts with their basic needs during periods of high stress. **Directions**: Mark the ways stress affects you, and then write in any additional neglected basic needs.

ACUTE (SYMPTOMS THAT OCCUR BEFORE OR DURING A STRESSFUL SITUATION)

Physical	Emotional/Cognitive	Behavioral
☐ Fatigue	☐ Irritability	☐ Substance use
☐ Indigestion	☐ Loss of motivation	☐ Interpersonal conflict
☐ Sweating	☐ Mood instability	☐ Teeth grinding
☐ Muscle tension	☐ Memory problems	☐ Recurring thoughts
☐ Asthma	☐ Decreased sex drive	☐ Procrastination
☐ Chest pain	☐ Difficulty concentrating	☐ Social withdrawal
☐ Nausea	☐ Anger/Frustration	☐ Over or Under eating
☐ Back pain	☐ Worry	☐ Sleep difficulties
☐ Headaches/Migraines		☐ Nail biting

CHRONIC (SYMPTOMS AND CONSEQUENCES OF LONG-TERM STRESS)

☐ Substance use	☐ Depression	☐ Heart disease
☐ Sleep disorders	☐ Memory impairment	☐ Weakened immune system
☐ Skin diseases	☐ Anxiety Disorders	
☐ Poor diet and exercise		

NEGLECTED BASIC NEEDS

☐ Social needs ☐ Personal hygiene ☐ Healthy diet ☐ Medical health
☐ Intimacy needs ☐ Sleep ☐ Exercise ☐ Mental health

_____

_____

STRESS MANAGEMENT

> The negative effects of stress can be reduced with the use of emotional management skills, social support, attending to basic needs, and maintaining a healthy life balance.

PRIORITIZE THE ESSENTIALS

Stress can trigger a harmful cycle where basic needs are overlooked, leading to even more stress. Make it a priority to consistently tend to your fundamental needs, especially during stressful times. This includes maintaining a balanced diet, exercising regularly, getting quality sleep, and practicing self-care. Remember to set aside time to relax and have fun every day, without interruptions.

TACKLE YOUR RESPONSIBILITIES

Start by addressing smaller tasks first. A long "to-do" list can feel overwhelming, even when the tasks are relatively simple. By taking care of the quick, easy items, you'll free up mental space and energy to concentrate on your larger responsibilities more effectively.

REMEMBER, STRESS ISN'T ALWAYS NEGATIVE

Stress can drive us to tackle challenges and find solutions. By viewing stress as a natural emotion or a useful tool, you can lessen many of its negative effects. The key is not to eliminate stress, but to manage it effectively and use it to your advantage.

SHARE YOUR CHALLENGES

Discussing your stressors, even without finding immediate solutions, can trigger hormones that alleviate the negative effects of stress. Spending time talking with friends and loved ones is important and beneficial, even when you're feeling overwhelmed.

KEEP A BALANCED APPROACH

Avoid placing all your focus on a single area of life. Those who concentrate too heavily on one aspect often struggle with stress when that area is at risk. Distribute your time and energy across multiple areas, such as family, career, hobbies, and friendships, to maintain a healthier balance and resilience.

KEEP THINGS IN PERSPECTIVE

When you are in the midst of high stress, little problems can feel bigger than they are. Take a step back, and think about how important your stressors are in a broader context. Writing about your stressors will help you develop a healthier perspective.

STRESS MANAGEMENT

Three people you can turn to for support:
1. _____
2. _____
3. _____

How they can help:
1. _____
2. _____
3. _____

How can you use your social support to ease one of your current stressors?

_____

_____

List two ways you have successfully handled unpleasant emotions in the past:

1. _____

2. _____

Describe ways you can protect your basic needs during periods of high stress.

_____

_____

_____

Areas of your life you would like to devote more attention to:
Select 3 areas

☐ Career   ☐ Education   ☐ Family   ☐ Intimacy
☐ Recreation/Fun ☐ Socializing   ☐ Spirituality   ☐ Other

I am okay right at this moment!

STRESS MANAGEMENT

> **Directions**: Describe things in your life that counteract stress. Put a checkmark next to or write in the positive experiences, actions, and characteristics in your life.

DAILY UPLIFTS (POSITIVE EXPERIENCES THAT MAKE YOU HAPPY)

- ☐ Leisure activities
- ☐ Eating a good meal
- ☐ Spending time with friends
- ☐ Spending time in nature
- ☐ Completing a task
- ☐ Spending time with family

_____

_____

HEALTHY COPING STRATEGIES (HELPS REDUCE OR MANAGE STRESS)

- ☐ Relaxation techniques
- ☐ Talking about problems
- ☐ Exercise
- ☐ Self-care
- ☐ Journaling
- ☐ Develop a routine

_____

_____

PROTECTIVE FACTORS (LIFE CIRCUMSTANCES THAT PROTECT YOU FROM STRESS)

- ☐ Good physical health
- ☐ Motivation to succeed
- ☐ Education
- ☐ Financial stability
- ☐ Supportive family
- ☐ Good social connections

_____

_____

I am an agent of change and acceptance!

MY PROTECTIVE FACTORS

Protective factors are elements that support mental well-being and help individuals stay resilient when facing challenges. The more protective factors someone has, the better they can navigate life's difficulties. **Directions**: Go through each protective factor below and use the scales to rate how well you think you're doing in each area.

SENSE OF PURPOSE

- Understanding personal values and living in line with them
- Meaningful engagement in activities & roles

0 1 2 3 4 5 6 7 8 9 10
Weak | Strong

PHYSICAL HEALTH

- Maintaining a balanced & healthy diet
- Following medical advice & treatment
- Getting enough exercise or staying active

0 1 2 3 4 5 6 7 8 9 10
Weak | Strong

COPING SKILLS

- Awareness of emotions & understanding how they affect your actions
- Managing difficult emotions in a healthy way

0 1 2 3 4 5 6 7 8 9 10
Weak | Strong

SELF-ESTEEM

- Acceptance of personal flaws, weaknesses, and mistakes
- Belief in ability to overcome challenges
- Belief in your self-worth

0 1 2 3 4 5 6 7 8 9 10
Weak | Strong

HEALTHY THINKING

- Ability to evaluate personal strengths and weaknesses logically
- Avoids dwelling on mistakes, flaws, or problems

0 1 2 3 4 5 6 7 8 9 10
Weak | Strong

SOCIAL SUPPORT

- Feelings of love, closeness, or friendship
- Ability to discuss issues
- People you can ask for practical support

0 1 2 3 4 5 6 7 8 9 10
Weak | Strong

I know I am resilient to stress!

WWW.GBADULTING.ORG

MY PROTECTIVE FACTORS

While some protective factors are beyond your control, many are within your reach. You have the power to choose who you surround yourself with, how you handle challenges, and how you spend your time each day. By concentrating on what you can control and strengthening those protective factors, you'll enhance your ability to navigate life's difficulties. **Directions**: Answer the following questions by referring to the previous page.

MOST VALUABLE PROTECTIVE FACTOR:

1. _____

HOW HAS THIS PROTECTIVE FACTOR BEEN HELPFUL?

_____
_____

PROTECTIVE FACTORS TO IMPROVE:

1. _____

2. _____

DESCRIBE THE BENEFITS OF IMPROVING THESE PROTECTIVE FACTORS.

_____
_____

LIST SPECIFIC STEPS OR ACTIONS TO ACHIEVE THESE GOALS.

_____
_____

COPING STRATEGIES

Coping strategies are the actions you use to manage stress, difficult emotions, or challenges. Unhealthy coping methods might provide temporary relief but can cause harm in the long run. On the other hand, healthy coping strategies may not offer immediate satisfaction, but they lead to lasting positive results. **Directions**: Identify and reflect on your healthy and unhealthy coping strategies.

UNHEALTHY COPING STRATEGIES

- Procrastination
- Overeating
- Drug or alcohol use
- Sleeping too little or too much
- Self-harm
- Aggression
- Social withdrawal

HEALTHY COPING STRATEGIES

- Problem-solving techniques
- Healthy eating
- Using social support
- Relaxation techniques
- Seeking professional help
- Exercise
- Talking about your problem

Describe a problem you are currently dealing with:

_____

_____

YOUR UNHEALTHY COPING STRATEGIES:

1. _____

2. _____

CONSEQUENCES OF UNHEALTHY COPING:

_____

_____

HEALTHY STRATEGIES YOU USE, OR COULD USE:

1. _____

2. _____

BARRIERS TO USING HEALTHY COPING STRATEGIES:

_____

_____

Peace is my strength!

HEALTHY COPING STRATEGIES

Keep an anger log	Play an instrument	Play with a pet
Cleaning	Call/Text a friend	Pay bills
Practice mindfulness	Professional development	Gardening
Practice yoga	Cook or Bake	Take a time-out
Listen to music	Deep breathing	Join a club/group
Tend to spirtual needs	Visit family	Challenge thoughts
Rearrange room	Plan a group event	Build new habits
Lift weights	Write or journal	Learn a language
Talk about it	Draw/Paint	Ask for support
Set boundaries	Problem solving	Positive self-talk
Create goals	Time management	Call a hotline
Invite a friend over	Create a to-do list	Face the problem

FEELINGS ABOUT: FINANCES

Money is a topic people normally do not talk about, so the impact that it has on a person's life is never truly understood. Complete this exercise to get a better understanding about your beliefs regarding money and finances. **Directions**: Indicate the feelings or behavior you identify with the most for each statement.

When it comes to financial planning, I prefer to...

| BUDGET | | | | | | WING IT |

My spending habits are...

| FRUGAL | | | | | | LAVISH |

My earliest memories about money are...

| UNPLEASANT | | | | | | PLEASANT |

When making a major purchase, I am...

| DEBT-AVERSE | | | | | | DEBT-WILLING |

Growing up, money was...

| SCARCE | | | | | | ABUNDANT |

When I have spare money, I tend to...

| SAVE | | | | | | SPEND |

When thinking about money, I focus on the...

| PRESENT | | | | | | FUTURE |

I prefer to spend money on...

| POSSESSIONS | | | | | | EXPERIENCES |

I can achieve financial stability & security!

FEELINGS ABOUT: FINANCES

I view financial success as a product of...

| HARD WORK | | | | | | LUCK |

In relationships, I prefer finances to be...

| SEPARATE | | | | | | MERGED |

When comparing my money situation with others, I feel...

| ENVIOUS | | | | | | CONTENT |

I prefer spending on...

| MYSELF | | | | | | OTHERS |

When I think about my financial future, I am...

| PESSIMISTIC | | | | | | OPTIMISTIC |

Most of my purchases are...

| PLANNED | | | | | | SPONTANEOUS |

When making financial decisions, I am...

| RISK-AVERSE | | | | | | RISK-TOLERANT |

I view money as a source of...

| STRESS | | | | | | ENJOYMENT |

I am worthy of financial abundance!

MONEY OVERVIEW

Becoming more secure with your finances means understanding your finances, and knowing where you stand financially. **Directions**: Fill out the following sections with real numbers. Do not give estimates.

Today's Date _____

EXPENSES

Due Date	Expense/Bill	Amount
		$
		$
		$
		$
		$
		$
		$
		$
		$
		$

Total Expenses: $_____

DEBTS

Debt	Amount
	$
	$
	$
	$
	$
	$
	$
	$
	$
	$

Total Debts: $_____

SAVINGS

Current Balance: $_____

INCOME

Total Income: $_____

GOALS

_____
_____

MONEY CHECK-IN

Directions: Come back to this page 6 months after completing the money overview worksheet. Fill out the following sections with real numbers, then reflect on your goals.

Today's Date

EXPENSES

DUE DATE	EXPENSE/BILL	AMOUNT
		$
		$
		$
		$
		$
		$
		$
		$
		$
		$

Total Expenses: $_____

DEBTS

DEBT	AMOUNT
	$
	$
	$
	$
	$
	$
	$
	$
	$
	$

Total Debts: $_____

SAVINGS

Current Balance: $_____

INCOME

Total Income: $_____

REFLECTION

_____
_____

EMERGENCY FUND TIPS

An emergency fund is a financial safety net for **unexpected expenses** like medical bills and losing your job. Aim to save at least three to six months worth of living expenses to give yourself a peace of mind and financial stability.

TIPS

- **Fund before other goals**
- **Create a realistic savings goal**
- **Cut back on non-essential spending**
- **Set a savings challenge**
- **Set up automatic transfers**
- **Open up a high-yield savings account**
- **Make paying off high-interest debt a priority**
- **Shop around for better prices**
    - Clothes
    - Car Insurance
    - Cellular/Internet plans
    - Anything else you buy
- **Cut back on unused streaming services, gym memberships, and other recurring expenses**
- **Pay with cash/debit not credit**
- **Start a side business or get a second job**
- **Sell extra items lying around**
- **Live within your means**
- **Avoid impulse buying**
- **Use your emergency fund for actual emergencies**
- **Monitor your progress**

I accept financial success!

EMERGENCY FUND TRACKER

Directions: Start off small by saving $1,000, then work towards saving 6 months worth of expenses. Set the amount that each block is worth, and mark when you have added the amount to your emergency fund. There are 100 blocks in total.

Fund Goal: $_____

Each Block Equals: $_____

CAREER PLANNING

Whether you are considering quitting your job, starting a career, or at risk for losing your job; this worksheet will help you create a solid plan to reach your goal. **Directions**: Fill out this worksheet thoroughly; being honest about your limitations, weaknesses, needs, and wants. Do the necessary research online, with yourself, and with others. Use this as a tool to push yourself further. Utilize this worksheet during your application and interview process to ensure your needs are being met.

REASON

☐ Quit   ☐ Start Career   ☐ Terminated

_____

_____

_____

_____

MOTIVATION

⓪ ① ② ③ ④ ⑤ ⑥ ⑦ ⑧ ⑨ ⑩
Not at all   Very

_____

_____

_____

_____

BENEFITS I MUST HAVE (MARK YOUR TOP 3 REQUIREMENTS)

☐ Health/Vision/Dental Insurance
☐ Relocation Assistance
☐ Health Club Membership
☐ Education Incentives
☐ Domestic/International Travel
☐ Paid Time Off (PTO)
   ☐ Unlimited
☐ Employee Stock Purchase Plan

☐ Retirement
   ☐ Matched
☐ Paid Family Leave
☐ Life Insurance
☐ Fertility Assistance
☐ Paid Parental Leave

☐ Other: _____

WORK PREFERENCES (MARK YOUR TOP 5)

☐ Permanent work
☐ Full-time work
☐ Part-time work
☐ Temporary work

☐ Close supervision
☐ Some supervision
☐ Little supervision
☐ Supervise others

☐ Work alone
☐ Work with others
☐ Remote
☐ Salary

☐ Day shift
☐ Evening shift
☐ Overnight
☐ Other: _____

Career Planning

Strengths

_____

_____

_____

Weaknesses

_____

_____

_____

Limitations

_____

_____

_____

Values

_____

_____

_____

CAREER PLANNING

	CURRENT	GOAL
POSITION		
COMPENSATION		
SKILLS	1. _____ 2. _____ 3. _____	1. _____ 2. _____ 3. _____
TRAINING	1. _____ 2. _____ 3. _____	1. _____ 2. _____ 3. _____

	COURSE	TIME	COST	
SKILLS GOAL				☐
				☐
				☐

	DEGREE/CERTIFICATE	TIME	COST	
TRAINING GOAL				☐
				☐
				☐

CONFIDENCE ⓪ ① ② ③ ④ ⑤ ⑥ ⑦ ⑧ ⑨ ⑩
Not at all   Very

REFLECTION POINT: CAREER

Exercise: Make sure you are in a comfortable space, free of distractions. Describe your dream job. Think about the jobs you would like to apply to. If you are willing to relocate to a new city, state, or country; write those places down. What kind of career would you like? What kind of life do you want to live? Do you have what it takes to get to where you want to be? If not, what will it take for you to get there? Be honest and detailed.

_____
_____
_____
_____
_____
_____
_____
_____
_____
_____
_____
_____
_____

APPLY TO THESE JOBS

1. _____
2. _____
3. _____

WILLING TO RELOCATE TO

1. _____
2. _____
3. _____

I accomplish my goals with tenacity!

CAREER PLANNING

- Update resume
- Create or update LinkedIn Profile
- Join Facebook groups
- Make new contacts
- Reach out to network
- Practice interview questions
- Audit social media profiles
- Follow-up after interview
- Attend a job fair
- Complete trainings
- Job search
- Update portfolio
- Attend interview
- Write cover letter
- Attend a conference
- Build brand

DATE	ACTIVITY	
		☐
		☐
		☐
		☐
		☐
		☐
		☐
		☐
		☐
		☐
		☐
		☐

I am focused and productive in my tasks!

FEELINGS ABOUT: HEALTH

Everyone's beliefs about health and health conditions play a role in determining their health related behaviors. Beliefs can be the reason why a person chooses to seek help or not to. **Directions**: Indicate the feelings or behavior you identify with the most for each statement.

When I think about my overall health, I believe that it is...

| POOR | | | | | EXCELLENT |

When I think about my mental or emotional health, I believe that it is...

| POOR | | | | | EXCELLENT |

To me, being healthy means...

| DISEASE-FREE | | | | | WELL-BEING |

When I feel unwell, I...

| SEEK HELP | | | | | SELF MEDICATE |

When I talk to a doctor or nurse, I give them all of the information they need to help me...

| NEVER | | | | | ALL OF THE TIME |

When I talk to a doctor or nurse, I ask the questions I need to ask...

| NEVER | | | | | ALL OF THE TIME |

When I talk to a doctor or nurse, I make sure they explain anything I do not understand...

| NEVER | | | | | ALL OF THE TIME |

Within the last 12 months, I have taken action to do something about my health

| NEVER | | | | | ALL OF THE TIME |

I love and respect my body!

FEELINGS ABOUT: HEALTH

My relationship with food and nutrition is...

| CHALLENGING | | | | | | GREAT |

When it comes to staying active, I feel...

| FRUSTRATED | | | | | | CONFIDENT |

The biggest challenge I face in maintaining my health is...

| MOTIVATION | | | | | | CONSISTENCY |

I see a healthcare provider for check-ups or preventative care...

| NEVER | | | | | | REGULARLY |

My feelings about using alternative or holistic approaches to health care are...

| PESSIMISTIC | | | | | | OPTIMISTIC |

When I think about sleep and its impact on my health, I believe it is...

| IRRELEVANT | | | | | | ESSENTIAL |

I manage stress and anxiety by...

| AVOIDING IT | | | | | | FACING IT |

I will advocate for my health!

WEEKLY FITNESS PLANNER

Month		Week

Monday Exercises:

Tuesday Exercises:

Wednesday Exercises:

Thursday Exercises:

Friday Exercises:

Saturday Exercises:

Sunday Exercises:

Weekly Goals

☐ _____

☐ _____

☐ _____

☐ _____

My Motivation

Notes/Reminders

Each goal brings me closer to my ideal self!

EMERGENCY PLAN

When we are in crisis, it is hard for us to remember exactly what we should do. Use the next couple of pages to help develop an emergency plan. **Directions**: Fill out this worksheet and post it in a highly visible area. **Call 911 in an emergency.**

EMERGENCY CONTACTS

NAME	PHONE NUMBER	RELATION
NAME	PHONE NUMBER	RELATION
NAME	PHONE NUMBER	RELATION
DOCTOR'S NAME	PHONE NUMBER	EMAIL ADDRESS

IMPORTANT INFORMATION

ALLERGIES

MEDICAL CONDITIONS

MEDICATIONS   BLOOD TYPE

EMERGENCY INFORMATION

LOCATION OF FIRST AID KIT   LOCATION OF EMERGENCY KIT

POLICE   FIRE   POISON CONTROL

EMERGENCY PLAN: DISASTER KIT

SUPPLIES

- ☐ Water (1 gallon per person per day)
- ☐ Food (non-perishable food)
- ☐ Battery-powered or hand crank radio
- ☐ Flashlight
- ☐ First aid kit
- ☐ Extra batteries
- ☐ Whistle
- ☐ Dust mask
- ☐ Plastic sheeting, scissors, & duct tape
- ☐ Moist towelettes
- ☐ Garbage bags
- ☐ Important documents

- ☐ Wrench or pliers
- ☐ Manual can opener
- ☐ Local maps
- ☐ Cell phone with chargers & backup battery
- ☐ Soap, hand sanitizer, & disinfecting wipes
- ☐ Prescription medications
- ☐ Non-prescription medications
- ☐ Sleeping bag
- ☐ Matches in waterproof container
- ☐ Feminine & personal hygiene supplies
- ☐ Paper & pencil
- ☐ Change of clothes & comfortable shoes

MAINTAINING YOUR KIT

After assembling your kit remember to maintain it so it is ready when needed:

- Keep canned food in a cool, dry place.
- Store boxed food in tightly closed plastic or metal containers
- Replace expired items as needed
- Rotate water supply every six months
- Rotate canned goods every year
- Re-think your needs every year and update your kit as your needs change

In an emergency, list 3 safe places:

1. _____
2. _____
3. _____

KIT STORAGE LOCATIONS

Since you do not know where you will be when an emergency occurs, prepare supplies for home, work, and cars.

- **Home**: Keep this kit in a designated place and have it ready in case you have to leave your home quickly. Make sure everyone in your household knows where the kit is kept.
- **Work**: Be prepared to shelter at work for at least 24 hours. Your work kit should include food, water, and other necessities like medicines, as well as comfortable walking shoes, stored in a backpack.
- **Car**: In case you are stranded, keep a kit of emergency supplies in your car.

I believe in my ability to keep myself safe!

EMERGENCY PLAN: CAR

SUPPLIES

- ☐ Jumper cables
- ☐ Flares or reflective triangle
- ☐ Ice scraper
- ☐ Car cell phone charger
- ☐ Blanket
- ☐ Map
- ☐ Cat litter or sand (for better tire traction)

BEFORE EMERGENCIES, CHECK:

- ☐ Antifreeze levels
- ☐ Battery & ignition system
- ☐ Brakes
- ☐ Exhaust system
- ☐ Thermostat
- ☐ Fuel & air filters
- ☐ Heater & defroster
- ☐ Lights & flashing hazard lights
- ☐ Oil
- ☐ Windshield wipers & washer fluid level

CAR SAFETY TIPS

- Keep your gas tank full in case of evacuation or power outages.
- Do not drive through flooded areas. Six inches of water can cause a vehicle to lose control or possibly stall.
- If a power line falls on your car, stay inside until a trained person removes the wire.
- If it becomes hard to control the car, pull over, stop the car, and set the parking brake
- If the emergency could affect the stability of the roadway, then avoid overpasses, bridges, power lines, signs, and other hazards.

DO NOT...

- Leave the scene of the accident until all details have been resolved
- Do not admit fault or blame
- Don't sign anything from other vehicle driver or party
- Discuss details of accident with anyone except police officer(s)

ACCIDENT CHECKLIST

- ☐ Check for injuries. Call 911
- ☐ If damage to the vehicle(s) is minor, move cars to side of road to avoid blocking traffic
- ☐ Exchange contact/insurance information with other driver
- ☐ Collect contact information from witnesses
- ☐ Take pictures of damage of both vehicles and accident scene from different angles
- ☐ Sketch accident scene
- ☐ Obtain police information

EMERGENCY PLAN: OUT OF COUNTRY

CHECKLIST

☐ Passport
☐ Visas
☐ Travel Insurance

☐ Medications
☐ International Driving Permit
☐ Currency exchanged

BE PREPARED

- Check your passport expiration dates. Some countries require that your passport expiration date is at least six months away.
- Check with the embassy of your destination regarding visa requirements.
- Make copies of all your travel documents. Leave one copy with a trusted friend or relative, and carry the other separately from your original documents. Take a picture of your travel documents with your phone to have an electronic copy.
- Some prescription drugs and some U.S. over-the-counter medications are illegal in other countries. Check the embassy of your destination about regulations and documentation before you travel.
- Many countries do not recognize a U.S. driver's license, but most accept an **International Driving Permit (IDP)**. You may also need supplemental car insurance.
- Check your health care policy to see if it will cover you overseas. If not, consider buying supplemental insurance. Make sure the insurance you purchase covers any special needs or risks you anticipate on your trip.
- Notify your bank and credit card companies of your travel, and check exchange rates.
- Enroll in the **Smart Traveler Enrollment Program (STEP)** to receive travel and security updates about your destination, and be contacted in case of an emergency.

BE SAFE

- Keep a list of your emergency contacts handy and create a communication plan for reaching family and friends in the event of a crisis.
- Phone lines may be affected during a crisis. Think about other ways to communicate. For example, update your social media status often and send messages as regularly as possible.
- Have an exit strategy. Know more than one way to get to safety without relying on help.
- Contact the nearest U.S. embassy or consulate if you need emergency help.

I trust in my own abilities and intuition!

GOAL CHECKPOINT

Long-Term Goal 1

Target Date	I REACHED MY GOAL	Still Relevant?	Still Achievable?
_____	☐	☐ Yes ☐ No	☐ Yes ☐ No

How can I maintain this goal: _____

_____

_____

_____

Long-Term Goal 2

Target Date	I REACHED MY GOAL	Still Relevant?	Still Achievable?
_____	☐	☐ Yes ☐ No	☐ Yes ☐ No

How can I maintain this goal: _____

_____

_____

_____

Long-Term Goal 3

Target Date	I REACHED MY GOAL	Still Relevant?	Still Achievable?
_____	☐	☐ Yes ☐ No	☐ Yes ☐ No

How can I maintain this goal: _____

_____

_____

_____

I embrace my true potential, free of limits!

GOAL CHECKPOINT

Area of Focus
☐ The Basic Boy
☐ The Safe & Secured Boy
☐ The Loved & Connected Boy
☐ The Confident Boy
☐ The Purposefully Driven Boy

Area of Focus

☐ Food	☐ Health	☐ Community
☐ Water	☐ Safety	☐ Esteem
☐ Shelter	☐ Social	☐ Status
☐ Sleep	☐ Family	☐ Recognition
☐ Finances	☐ Friends	☐ Purpose
☐ Authenticity	☐ Creativity	☐ Development

New Long-Term Goal

How **important** is it that you make this change?   ⓪ ① ② ③ ④ ⑤ ⑥ ⑦ ⑧ ⑨ ⑩
Not at all · · · Very

Short-Term Goal 1

How **confident** are you that you are able to make this change?   ⓪ ① ② ③ ④ ⑤ ⑥ ⑦ ⑧ ⑨ ⑩
Not at all · · · Very

How **important** is it that you make this change?   ⓪ ① ② ③ ④ ⑤ ⑥ ⑦ ⑧ ⑨ ⑩
Not at all · · · Very

I REACHED MY GOAL THIS WEEK!   1 ☐ 2 ☐ 3 ☐ 4 ☐ 5 ☐ 6 ☐ 7 ☐ 8 ☐

Short-Term Goal 2

How **confident** are you that you are able to make this change?   ⓪ ① ② ③ ④ ⑤ ⑥ ⑦ ⑧ ⑨ ⑩
Not at all · · · Very

How **important** is it that you make this change?   ⓪ ① ② ③ ④ ⑤ ⑥ ⑦ ⑧ ⑨ ⑩
Not at all · · · Very

I REACHED MY GOAL THIS WEEK!   1 ☐ 2 ☐ 3 ☐ 4 ☐ 5 ☐ 6 ☐ 7 ☐ 8 ☐

Short-Term Goal 3

How **confident** are you that you are able to make this change?   ⓪ ① ② ③ ④ ⑤ ⑥ ⑦ ⑧ ⑨ ⑩
Not at all · · · Very

How **important** is it that you make this change?   ⓪ ① ② ③ ④ ⑤ ⑥ ⑦ ⑧ ⑨ ⑩
Not at all · · · Very

I REACHED MY GOAL THIS WEEK!   1 ☐ 2 ☐ 3 ☐ 4 ☐ 5 ☐ 6 ☐ 7 ☐ 8 ☐

My belief in myself is unshakeable!

I choose people in my life who make me feel safe!

The Loved & Connected Boy

Building connections with others can be a very difficult task. In order to have healthy relationships, there are some aspects that need to be maintained. This section will give you tools to create those relationships.

MY SUPPORT SYSTEM

Your support system includes the help you receive from family, friends, groups, or communities, and it can meet a variety of needs. Having a strong support network can boost your physical health, self-esteem, mental well-being, and enhance feelings of security, life satisfaction, and resilience to stress. **Directions**: Follow the prompts to complete the worksheet.

EMOTIONAL SUPPORT

- Assist in managing emotions. This helps with handling emotions like stress, anger, or depression. It often involves listening to your concerns and offering empathy.

TANGIBLE SUPPORT

- Help with practical issues. This type of help addresses practical needs, such as offering financial assistance, providing transportation to work, or childcare.

INFORMATIONAL SUPPORT

- Offer problem-solving information. This involves providing guidance to help tackle a problem or overcome a challenge, such as advice or sharing useful resources.

SOCIAL NEEDS

- Address basic social needs. This support helps meet essential social needs like love, belonging, and connection, fostering a sense of security and contentment.

Your support system:

1. _____

2. _____

3. _____

Describe ways each of your supports help you, or could help you:

1. _____

2. _____

3. _____

I deserve fulfilling relationships!

MY SUPPORT SYSTEM

BUILDING YOUR SUPPORT SYSTEM

- **Nurture your existing relationships.** Connect with friends and family. Make it a priority to stay in touch with your closest relationships, even when other parts of your life get busy.
- **Boost your community engagement.** Get more involved in hobby groups, volunteering, or religious groups. It's a fantastic way to connect with like-minded individuals and build a new support network.
- **Seek professional support.** Turn to doctors, therapists, and other professionals for help with complex problems or challenges that are too difficult to handle on your own.
- **Attend support groups.** Connect with others who are dealing with similar problems or life experiences. It can be rewarding to share your own story and provide support to others.

Barriers to using your support:

1. _____
2. _____
3. _____

Steps to take to utilize your support:

1. _____
2. _____
3. _____

How can your support help with a current problem:

1. _____
2. _____
3. _____

I attract positive & supportive relationships!

FRIENDSHIP RITUAL

Sometimes life can get in the way of nurturing our friendships. When we create friendship rituals, it allows us to strengthen connections and create lasting memories. Use the tips and ideas below to create your own friendship ritual.

TIPS FOR FRIENDSHIP RITUALS

- **Make it a priority.** Protect the time you set aside for your ritual, even when life gets busy.
- **Be completely present.** Spend your time mindfully, focusing on your friend and the experience you are sharing.
- **Eliminate distractions.** Turn off the TV, silence your phone, and move away from any other distractions.
- **Keep it simple.** A ritual does not have to be a big event. It can be as simple as watching a show together.
- **Do it consistently.** Make a habit of doing the ritual as often as possible.

IDEAS FOR FRIENDSHIP RITUALS

BOOK CLUB

- Choose a book, podcast, or other media to share. You can read or listen separately, but come together afterwards to discuss.

WORKOUT TOGETHER

- Bond over a small group workout session by breaking a sweat. Try a new fitness class, running club, or yoga.

GAME NIGHT

- Choose a board game or a deck of cards and have a game night with your friends. You can choose to keep it lighthearted or use this time to create a stronger bond.

GO OUT TO EAT

- Dinner can be a little forced and a lunch meeting can feel like a business meeting, but brunch is the perfect time to spend time with friends.

ADVENTURE ACTIVITIES

- Fishing, go-karting, inner-tubing, jet-skiing, and other adventurous activities can be great ways to bond with friends.

VIDEO GAMES

- Having a night in and hopping on a gaming console can be an easy way to bond with friends virtually.

I attract lasting friendships!

MY LOVE LANGUAGE HIERARCHY

Love languages are the different ways we express and receive love. Knowing your own love language, as well as those of the people you care about, helps make sharing your feelings easier and more meaningful. **Directions**: Label each love language as a hierarchy based on which one is most important to you (1) and which one is the least important (5).

GIFTS
1-5 ☐

- Giving a present
- Creating something (e.g. artwork)
- Buying flowers
- Other thoughtful surprises

Favorite examples:

_____

_____

QUALITY TIME
1-5 ☐

- Going on a date
- Having a nice conversation
- Eating together
- Being present

Favorite examples:

_____

_____

ACTS OF SERVICE
1-5 ☐

- Make their favorite treat or meal
- Cover a bill
- Run errands
- Other tasks that are beneficial

Favorite examples:

_____

_____

PHYSICAL TOUCH
1-5 ☐

- Holding hands
- Hugging
- Spending intimate time together
- Other affectionate touching

Favorite examples:

_____

_____

WORDS OF AFFIRMATION
1-5 ☐

- Giving encouragement
- Giving compliments
- Stating your feelings (e.g. "I love you")
- Sharing positive thoughts

Favorite examples:

_____

_____

EXPLORING ATTACHMENT STYLES

Attachment styles describe how individuals think about and behave in relationships. Formed in childhood, these styles significantly influence how we experience and manage relationships throughout our lives. **Directions**: Choose a value between 1 and 10, 1 being "not at all", and 10 being "all the time."

SECURE

I have the ability to regulate my emotions.	☐☐☐☐☐☐☐☐☐☐ 1 = Not at all All the time = 10
I have the ability to seek emotional support when I need it.	☐☐☐☐☐☐☐☐☐☐ 1 = Not at all All the time = 10
I am able to manage conflict well.	☐☐☐☐☐☐☐☐☐☐ 1 = Not at all All the time = 10
I trust others easily.	☐☐☐☐☐☐☐☐☐☐ 1 = Not at all All the time = 10
I am easy to connect with.	☐☐☐☐☐☐☐☐☐☐ 1 = Not at all All the time = 10
I am comfortable being alone.	☐☐☐☐☐☐☐☐☐☐ 1 = Not at all All the time = 10
I have the ability to be emotionally available.	☐☐☐☐☐☐☐☐☐☐ 1 = Not at all All the time = 10

AVOIDANT

I find myself avoiding emotional or physical intimacy.	☐☐☐☐☐☐☐☐☐ 1 = Not at all All the time = 10
I am dismissive of others.	☐☐☐☐☐☐☐☐☐ 1 = Not at all All the time = 10
I feel threatened by anyone who tries to get close to me.	☐☐☐☐☐☐☐☐☐ 1 = Not at all All the time = 10
I feel I have commitment issues.	☐☐☐☐☐☐☐☐☐☐ 1 = Not at all All the time = 10

No one can determine my worth, except me!

EXPLORING ATTACHMENT STYLES

ANXIOUS

I tend to get very clingy in relationships.	☐☐☐☐☐☐☐☐☐☐ 1 = Not at all · All the time = 10
I tend to get very jealous in relationships.	☐☐☐☐☐☐☐☐☐☐ 1 = Not at all · All the time = 10
I have an intense fear of being rejected.	☐☐☐☐☐☐☐☐☐☐ 1 = Not at all · All the time = 10
I have feelings that I am unworthy of being loved.	☐☐☐☐☐☐☐☐☐☐ 1 = Not at all · All the time = 10
I have a significant fear of being abandoned.	☐☐☐☐☐☐☐☐☐☐ 1 = Not at all · All the time = 10
I am highly sensitive to criticism, whether it is real or perceived.	☐☐☐☐☐☐☐☐☐☐ 1 = Not at all · All the time = 10
I have a difficult time being alone.	☐☐☐☐☐☐☐☐☐☐ 1 = Not at all · All the time = 10

DISORGANIZED

I have a negative view of myself.	☐☐☐☐☐☐☐☐☐☐ 1 = Not at all · All the time = 10
I find myself desperately seeking love, but push partners away because of my fear for love.	☐☐☐☐☐☐☐☐☐☐ 1 = Not at all · All the time = 10
I have a difficult time effectively communicating my needs to others.	☐☐☐☐☐☐☐☐☐☐ 1 = Not at all · All the time = 10
I find myself being both independent and clingy in relationships.	☐☐☐☐☐☐☐☐☐☐ 1 = Not at all · All the time = 10
I have high levels of anxiety.	☐☐☐☐☐☐☐☐☐☐ 1 = Not at all · All the time = 10
I am fearful of getting close to people.	☐☐☐☐☐☐☐☐☐☐ 1 = Not at all · All the time = 10
I feel that I do not deserve a healthy relationship.	☐☐☐☐☐☐☐☐☐☐ 1 = Not at all · All the time = 10

ATTACHMENT STYLES

INSECURE

AVOIDANT

Often seems aloof and emotionally disengaged, avoiding intimacy, vulnerability, and commitment. Tends to spend time apart from their partner or friends.	• Uncomfortable with emotions and conflict • Difficulty expressing needs and wants • Extremely rigid, protective, & distant

ANXIOUS

Concerned about their partner's or friend's availability and commitment. Often feels incomplete without them and may seek constant reassurance or struggle with jealousy.	• Fearful of abandonment, rejection, and conflict • Sensitive to criticism and seeking approval • Mistrustful of partners or friends and relationships

DISORGANIZED

Switches between anxious and avoidant attachment styles. Often desires intimacy but also distrusts it, leading to conflicting and inconsistent behavior with their partner.	• Struggles with maintaining healthy boundaries • Experiences high-conflict relationships • Prone to emotional extremes

SECURE

Satisfying and healthy relationships with strong intimacy, good communication, and mutual autonomy. Can clearly express needs and trusts their partner/friends.	• Committed to relationships, but independent • Attentive, affectionate, and accepting • Able to handle and resolve conflict

CREATING SECURE ATTACHMENT

- **Understand your attachment style.** This insight helps you identify patterns in your relationship history and develop strategies to change unproductive behaviors.
- **Counteract your anxious or avoidant tendencies.** If you have an anxious attachment style, work on becoming more independent in small steps. If you have an avoidant attachment style, try lowering your defenses and initiating intimacy.
- **Reflect on your beliefs about relationships.** Early life experiences often shape these views, so it's important to assess what is truly happening in your current relationships and

ATTACHMENT STYLES

let go of outdated beliefs and interpretations.

- **Reduce stressors.** Stress can exacerbate attachment issues. Take a proactive approach by focusing on self-care, addressing conflicts early, and participating in calming activities with your partner or friends.
- **Boost your emotional awareness.** Developing the ability to express and manage your own emotions enhances your capacity to understand and empathize with the emotions of your partner or friends. This reduces reactivity and strengthens attachment security.
- **Listen with empathy and communicate openly.** Secure attachment relies on respectful and heartfelt communication. During conflicts, work together with your partner or friends to ensure both of you feel understood and connected, even if you have differing views
- **Surround yourself with people who have healthy relationships.** Just as being around successful runners can help you train for a marathon, observing and learning from those with healthy relationships can enhance your own relationship skills and behaviors.

MORE INFORMATION

- Early parenting, childhood experiences, and adult interactions all contribute to shaping your attachment style.
- Partners or friends can impact each other's attachment styles, either positively or negatively.
- While most people have a primary attachment style, it's common to exhibit traits from other styles as well.
- Individuals with insecure attachment can move towards a more secure style by adopting new beliefs and behaviors.

I can give myself the reassurance that I need!

RELATIONSHIP GREEN FLAGS

Every relationship is unique. Green flags in relationships are positive traits and behaviors. In healthy relationships, individuals demonstrate appreciation, respect boundaries, and collaborate effectively to resolve issues. **Directions**: Mark areas that need improvement.

SELF-CONFIDENCE
- You feel comfortable being yourself.

INTIMACY
- You feel connected and close to your partner/friend, physically & emotionally.

SAFETY
- You honor boundaries and feel safe physically, intellectually, & emotionally.

INDEPENDENCE
- You have your own interests and goals.

APPRECIATION
- You respect and value your partner/friend, and frequently express gratitude.

BALANCE
- You find fulfillment in time spent together and apart.

EMPATHY
- You consider your partner's/friend's perspective and understand their feelings.

HONESTY
- You are genuine. Your actions consistently match your words.

CONFLICT RESOLUTION
- You own your actions and collaborate as a team to solve problems.

EFFECTIVE COMMUNICATION
- You express your needs and desires while honoring those of others.

COMMITMENT
- You are committed and dedicate sufficient time and energy to the relationship.

COMMONALITY
- You and your partner/friend share meaningful goals, beliefs, and values.

WWW.GBADULTING.ORG

GASLIGHTING WARNING SIGNS

Gaslighting is a form of manipulation that makes someone question their own beliefs, memory, or sanity. Recognizing the warning signs can help you better resist this type of manipulation.

DISTRACTION

- The gaslighter interrupts/shifts the subject to avoid addressing the victim's points.

While discussing an important issue: "Let's plan a trip!"

SABOTAGE

- The gaslighter deliberately undermines the victim to make them appear incompetent.

Throwing away the victim's mail so they cannot pay a bill on time.

DENIAL

- The gaslighter denies the victim's memory of an event or conversation, saying it either never happened or occurred differently.

"I never said that."

THREATS

- The gaslighter threatens negative consequences if the victim doesn't trust them or accept their version of events.

"If you cannot see things my way, this relationship is over."

PUT-DOWNS

- The gaslighter belittles and criticizes the victim, causing them to doubt themselves.

"You're an idiot. You have no clue what you're saying."

MINIMIZATION

- The gaslighter downplays or trivializes a serious situation or accusation.

"Whatever, it was nothing."

IGNORING/AVOIDANCE

- The gaslighter avoids engaging in conversation or acknowledging the victim's concerns.

Turning up the volume on the TV.

PROJECTION

- The gaslighter projects their own behavior onto the victim, accusing them of doing exactly what they themselves are doing.

"Maybe you're the one who's hiding something."

BOUNDARY STYLES & TYPES

Boundaries are the personal rules and limits we establish within relationships. They define what is acceptable and what isn't. It's normal to have different boundary styles in various relationships.

BOUNDARY STYLES

RIGID	HEALTHY	POROUS
• Maintains distance from most people • Avoids intimacy and close connections • Frequently says "no" to others • Disregards others' opinions • Communicates in an aggressive manner • Rarely seeks help • Distrustful of others • Keeps personal information tightly guarded • Avoids conflict by pushing people away • Holds rigid, inflexible personal values	• Chooses carefully whom to let in or keep out • Values their own opinions • Can say "no" when necessary • Respects both their own and others' opinions • Communicates assertively • Takes time to build trust with others • Shares personal information appropriately • Views conflict as a natural part of life • Upholds personal values while remaining flexible	• Allows almost anyone to get close • Tolerates abuse or disrespect • Struggles to say "no" to others • Easily swayed by others' opinions • Communicates passively • Excessively trusts others, including strangers • Shares personal information excessively • Avoids conflict by yielding to others • Fails to assert personal values • Fears rejection if they don't comply with others

MORE INFORMATION

- The suitability of boundaries varies by context. For example, what you feel comfortable sharing with friends might not be appropriate in a workplace setting.
- Many people exhibit a blend of different boundary styles; someone might have healthy boundaries with family, more porous boundaries at work, and a mix of all three types in their romantic relationships.

I am the main character in my life!

Boundary Styles & Types

Boundary Types

Physical

- **Personal space and physical touch**. Healthy boundaries involve recognizing what is appropriate in different settings and relationships (e.g., a hug, handshake, or kiss). Physical boundaries can be crossed if someone touches you without your consent or invades your personal space, such as by rummaging through your bedroom.

Intellectual

- **Thoughts and ideas.** Healthy intellectual boundaries involve respecting others' ideas and knowing what topics are appropriate for discussion (e.g., weather versus politics). These boundaries are crossed when someone dismisses or belittles another person's thoughts or opinions.

Emotional

- **Feelings.** Healthy emotional boundaries involve knowing when to share personal information and when to keep it private. For instance, gradually revealing personal details as a relationship develops, rather than disclosing everything to everyone. These boundaries are breached when someone criticizes, belittles, or invalidates another person's feelings.

Sexual

- **Emotional, intellectual, and physical aspects of sexuality.** Healthy sexual boundaries require mutual understanding and respect for each partner's limitations and desires. These boundaries are breached through unwanted sexual touch, pressure to participate in sexual activities, inappropriate staring, or sexual remarks.

Material

- **Money and possessions**. Healthy material boundaries involve establishing limits on what you are willing to share and with whom. For instance, it might be acceptable to lend a car to a family member, but not to someone you just met. These boundaries are breached when someone steals or damages another person's belongings, or pressures them to give or lend their possessions.

Time

- **Use of time.** To maintain healthy time boundaries, a person needs to allocate sufficient time for various aspects of their life, such as work, relationships, and hobbies. These boundaries are violated when someone demands excessive amounts of another person's time.

REFLECTION POINT: BOUNDARIES

Exercise: Make sure you are in a comfortable space, free of distractions. Add a check in the appropriate column for each boundary category. Think about who you struggle to set healthy boundaries with (e.g. friends, partner, family, coworkers). Take a moment to imagine what it would be like when you begin to establish healthy boundaries with this person. What are some specific actions you can take to improve your boundaries? How do you think the person will respond to these changes? How do you think your life will be different once you establish healthy boundaries? Be honest and detailed.

BOUNDARY CATEGORY	RIGID	HEALTHY	POROUS
PHYSICAL			
INTELLECTUAL			
EMOTIONAL			
SEXUAL			
MATERIAL			
TIME			

_____

_____

_____

_____

_____

_____

_____

_____

_____

I protect my heart and mind fiercely!

SETTING BOUNDARIES

TIPS FOR HEALTHY BOUNDARIES

- **Recognize your personal limits.** Before getting involved in any situation, clearly define what is acceptable to you and what isn't. Being specific helps prevent the gradual erosion of your boundaries, where you might end up giving more and more until you've given too much.
- **Understand what matters to you.** Base your boundaries on your personal values—what matters most to you. For instance, if you value family time, set firm boundaries against working late.
- **Pay attention to your feelings.** Pay attention to your feelings rather than suppressing them. Resentment often stems from feeling taken advantage of.
- **Value and honor yourself.** If you consistently yield to others, reflect on whether you're showing yourself the same respect you extend to them. Overly flexible boundaries might result from a misguided desire to be liked, putting others' needs before your own.
- **Show consideration for others.** Ensure your actions aren't self-serving at others' expense. Interactions should focus on fairness, considering the context and relationships involved. Winning at the expense of long-term relationship health isn't beneficial.
- **Speak up confidently..** When it's time to set a boundary, be clear and respectful. Firmly say "no" if necessary, but be open to compromise if it respects your boundaries. This approach can help soften the refusal while showing consideration for everyone involved.
- **Take a broader perspective.** Understand that there will be times when you give more and times when you take more. Be open to a broader perspective on relationships, but if you find yourself always giving or always taking, there may be an issue.

HOW TO SAY NO

"This doesn't work for me"	"I'm not comfortable with this"	"I do not want to do that"
"Please don't do that"	"This is not acceptable"	"Not at this time"
"I can't do that for you"	"I've decided not to"	"I'm drawing the line at __"

I confidently say no, when I need rest!

SETTING BOUNDARIES

Directions: Respond to the following questions as if you were really in each situation. Think about the language you would use to firmly state your boundary.

Situation: Your sister asks if you can watch her two young children on Saturday morning. You already have plans.

_____

_____

Situation: You notice your roommate has been eating your food in the fridge. You never discussed plans to share food, and don't want them eating what you bought.

_____

_____

Situation: A good friend asks you out on a date. You are not interested in being more than friends. You would like to let them down clearly, but gently.

_____

_____

Situation: Your friend calls you at 11pm to discuss issues she is having with her boyfriend. You need to wake up at 6 am.

_____

_____

Situation: You missed several days of work due to a medical condition. When you get back, a coworker asks what happened. You feel this information is personal, and do not want to share.

_____

_____

It's okay to change my mind at any time!

WWW.GBADULTING.ORG

COMMUNICATION

Directions: Respond to the following questions as if you were really in each situation. Think about the language you would use to communicate assertively.

COMMUNICATION STYLES

PASSIVE	ASSERTIVE	AGGRESSIVE
• Soft-spoken or reserved • Tends to let others take advantage • Puts others' needs first • Limited eye contact or looks away • Fails to communicate personal needs or desires • Lacks confidence	• Listens attentively without interrupting • Clearly communicates needs and desires • Open to compromises • Advocates for their own rights • Displays confidence with tone and body language • Maintains strong eye contact	• Quick to become frustrated • Uses a loud or aggressive tone • Refuses to compromise • Employs criticism, humiliation, or control • Often interrupts or fails to listen • Shows disrespect toward others

TIPS FOR ASSERTIVENESS

- **Respect yourself.** Your needs, wants, and rights are just as important as anyone else's. It's completely acceptable to communicate your desires, as long as you remain considerate of others' rights.
- **Express yourself calmly.** Avoid giving the silent treatment, yelling, threatening, or shaming. Take ownership of your emotions and share them in a calm, factual manner. Try using phrases like "I feel..." to articulate your thoughts and feelings.
- **Plan what to say.** Before entering a conversation, clarify your wants and needs and how you'll express them. Plan specific phrases and words to use during the discussion.
- **Say "no" when necessary.** You can't please everyone all the time. When you need to decline something, do so clearly and honestly, without fabricating reasons. If possible, suggest alternative solutions.

Situation: A friend asks to borrow your car. This will be a big inconvenience for you.

_____

_____

COMMUNICATION

Situation: You are working on a group project, and one member is not completing their portion. You have repeatedly had to finish their work.

_____

_____

Situation: A friend always cancels plans at the last minute. Recently, you were waiting for them at a restaurant, when they called to say they could not make it.

_____

_____

Situation: Your boss keeps dumping new work on you, with little instruction, and not enough time. Despite working overtime, you're weeks behind.

_____

_____

Situation: You've just received your food at a restaurant, and it was prepared incorrectly. Your sandwich seems to have extra pickles, instead of no pickles.

_____

_____

Situation: A friend showed up at your house uninvited. Usually you would be happy to let them in, but this time you're busy.

_____

_____

No is a complete sentence!

GOAL CHECKPOINT

Long-Term Goal 1

Target Date | I REACHED MY GOAL | Still Relevant? ☐ Yes ☐ No | Still Achievable? ☐ Yes ☐ No ☐

How can my support system help me with this goal : _____

Long-Term Goal 2

Target Date | I REACHED MY GOAL | Still Relevant? ☐ Yes ☐ No | Still Achievable? ☐ Yes ☐ No ☐

How can my support system help me with this goal : _____

Long-Term Goal 3

Target Date | I REACHED MY GOAL | Still Relevant? ☐ Yes ☐ No | Still Achievable? ☐ Yes ☐ No ☐

How can my support system help me with this goal : _____

I prioritize my needs and protect my peace!

I am brave enough to face my fears and challenges!

THE CONFIDENT BOY

Being confident in yourself requires you to know yourself. It takes a lot of self-compassion. This section is all about you. You will take a deep dive into knowing what it means to be you in all aspects of life.

MY LIFE STORY

Writing a personal story can help you discover meaning and value in your experiences. It provides an opportunity to organize your thoughts and use them for personal growth. People who create narratives about their lives often find a deeper sense of purpose, which can enhance their overall happiness.

THE PAST

WRITE THE STORY OF YOUR PAST. BE SURE TO DESCRIBE CHALLENGES YOU'VE OVERCOME, AND THE PERSONAL STRENGTHS THAT ALLOWED YOU TO DO SO.

_____

_____

_____

_____

_____

_____

_____

_____

_____

_____

_____

_____

_____

_____

_____

_____

_____

_____

_____

_____

MY LIFE STORY

THE PRESENT

DESCRIBE YOUR LIFE AND WHO YOU ARE NOW. HOW DO YOU DIFFER FROM YOUR PAST SELF? WHAT ARE YOUR STRENGTHS NOW? WHAT CHALLENGES ARE YOU FACING?

My Life Story

The Future

I AM...

Identity is how you perceive, describe, and present yourself. It encompasses various roles, traits, and experiences. A well-defined sense of identity can provide meaning and direction in life. **Directions**: Name the parts of your identity and describe what they mean to you. Then, rate how much you identify with each part (1 = very little, 10 = very strongly).

PART OF MY IDENTITY	RATING (1-10)

What it means to me:

_____

_____

_____

PART OF MY IDENTITY	RATING (1-10)

What it means to me:

_____

_____

_____

PART OF MY IDENTITY	RATING (1-10)

What it means to me:

_____

_____

_____

PART OF MY IDENTITY	RATING (1-10)

What it means to me:

_____

_____

_____

PART OF MY IDENTITY	RATING (1-10)

What it means to me:

_____

_____

_____

PART OF MY IDENTITY	RATING (1-10)

What it means to me:

_____

_____

_____

WRITE A TITLE OR NICKNAME FOR YOUR IDENTITY.

_____

MY CORE BELIEFS

Core beliefs are a person's fundamental views about themselves, others, and the world. They serve as a filter through which every situation and life experience is interpreted. As a result, individuals with different core beliefs may react, feel, and behave quite differently even when faced with the same circumstances.

SITUATION: TWO PEOPLE WITH DIFFERENT CORE BELIEFS GO THROUGH A BREAK-UP.

PERSON	CORE BELIEF	REACTION
A	"I will end up alone."	**Thought:** My ex did not want me, nobody will. **Feeling:** Depressed **Behavior:** Makes no changes
B	"I am loveable, and I have great qualities."	**Thought:** I did not spend enough time dating. **Feeling:** Disappointed **Behavior:** Plans to spend more time dating.

HARMFUL CORE BELIEFS

- **Helpless.** "I am weak". "I am a loser". "I am trapped".
- **Unlovable.** "I am unlovable". "No one likes me". "I am ugly".
- **Worthless.** "I am bad". "I don't deserve to live". "I am a failure". "I am worthless".
- **External danger.** "The world is dangerous". "People can't be trusted". "Nothing ever goes right".

CONSEQUENCES

- **Interpersonal problems.** Difficulty trusting others, feelings of inadequacy in relationships, excessive jealousy, overly confrontational or aggressive, putting others' needs above your own needs
- **Mental health problems.** Depression, anxiety, substance abuse, difficulty handling stress, low self-esteem

NOTE: NEGATIVE CORE BELIEFS ARE NOT NECESSARILY TRUE, EVEN IF THEY FEEL TRUE.

YOUR NEGATIVE CORE BELIEF:

LIST THREE PIECES OF EVIDENCE CONTRARY TO YOUR NEGATIVE CORE BELIEF.

1. _____
2. _____
3. _____

I focus on what I can control, and let go of the rest!

My Triggers

Triggers are stimuli such as people, places, situations, or things that provoke an unwanted emotional or behavioral response. To start identifying your own triggers, consider each of the categories listed below.

Trigger Categories

EMOTIONAL STATE: _____

PEOPLE: _____

PLACES: _____

THINGS: _____

THOUGHTS: _____

ACTIVITIES/SITUATIONS: _____

DESCRIBE YOUR THREE BIGGEST TRIGGERS, IN DETAIL.

1. _____
2. _____
3. _____

DESCRIBE YOUR STRATEGY FOR AVOIDING OR REDUCING EXPOSURE TO EACH TRIGGER.

1. _____
2. _____
3. _____

DESCRIBE YOUR STRATEGY FOR DEALING WITH EACH TRIGGER HEAD ON, WHEN THEY CANNOT BE AVOIDED.

1. _____
2. _____
3. _____

CHALLENGING NEGATIVE THOUGHTS

Depression, poor self-esteem, and anxiety are often the result of irrational negative thoughts. Challenging irrational thoughts can help change them.

What negative thought(s) am I having? _____

_____

_____

How does this negative thought make me feel? _____

_____

_____

Why am I having this negative thought? _____

_____

_____

Is there evidence for my thoughts? _____

_____

_____

Is there evidence contrary to my thought? _____

_____

_____

Am I attempting to interpret this situation without all the evidence? _____

_____

_____

CHALLENGING NEGATIVE THOUGHTS

Will this matter a year from now? How about five years from now? _____
_____
_____

What would a friend think about this situation? _____
_____
_____

If I look at the situation positively, how is it different? _____
_____
_____

What are the advantages and disadvantages of thinking this way? _____
_____
_____

Am I focusing only on the negative things? _____
_____
_____

Am I concentrating on my weaknesses instead of my strengths? _____
_____
_____

IMPOSTER SYNDROME

Imposter syndrome involves enduring feelings of inadequacy that don't align with reality or others' views. The main characteristic of imposter syndrome is a continual fear of being exposed as a fraud. While it's normal to occasionally feel out of place or doubt yourself, these feelings become problematic if they are persistent and pervasive.

TRAITS	CONSEQUENCES	RISK FACTORS
• Setting unrealistically high expectations for oneself • Fear of discovery as a fraud • Concealing shortcomings instead of addressing them • Frequently feeling out of place or inadequate • Focusing on negative feedback while overlooking praise and accomplishments	• Missed opportunities • Low self-esteem • Loss of confidence • Depression • Reduced productivity • Burnout • Social isolation • Anxiety	• Hostile or negative environment • Being the first in the family to assume a particular role • Childhood focused on achievement • Perfectionist tendencies • Facing discrimination or bias • Struggling with low self-esteem or self-defeating thoughts • Measuring success primarily by job role • Strong need for external validation

EXAMPLES

IN A RELATIONSHIP	AT WORK
After several unsatisfying relationships, Sabrina found someone who feels like a perfect fit. But she's plagued by feelings of inadequacy and unworthiness. Sabrina goes out of her way to hide her imperfections. She's convinced her partner will one day discover her flaws and leave her.	Patrick just started a new job. Everyone was impressed by his application, but Patrick agonizes over whether he can meet their expectations. He berates himself for any mistake, real or perceived, discounting anything he does well. He's terrified he'll be exposed as an incompetent fraud.

KEY FACTS

Women & underrepresented groups are more likely to experience imposter syndrome.	Around 70% of people have suffered from imposter syndrome at some point.	Imposter syndrome is common in high-achieving individuals.

I get stronger even on my weakest days!

IMPOSTER SYNDROME

TIPS FOR OVERCOMING IMPOSTER SYNDROME

- **Assess the evidence.** Making a list by collecting, acknowledging, and reflecting on proof of your competency can help combat imposter syndrome.
- **Refocus on values.** Take your focus away from outward signs of success or achievement and remind yourself of what really matters to you.
- **Reframe around growth.** Life and a career are a journey. You cannot grow, learn, or make progress without stretching yourself.
- **Get out of your head.** Rumination, a pattern of circling thoughts, goes hand-in-hand with imposter syndrome. Find someone to talk to or write down your fears, they are less powerful when they aren't circling.
- **Practice self-compassion.** Don't beat yourself up for feeling like a fraud. Now that you understand where the doubt and inadequacy come from, give yourself credit and compassion for how far you've come. You are a human. Humans make mistakes. You will too. Practicing self-compassion will help you tame your inner critic.
- **Keep failure in perspective.** Instead of focusing and defining your failure in the abstract, take time to write down the likely outcomes if some part of your effort fails. Rarely is it the end of the world. Try learning from your failures instead of letting your failures define you.
- **Practice mindfulness.** Take time to stop, breathe, notice your feelings, reassess, and respond. This technique gives you the opportunity to situate yourself in the present. It's a reflection point that enables you to recognize the capacities you have and used to successfully reach this point.

EVIDENCE THAT I AM INADEQUATE	EVIDENCE THAT I AM COMPETENT

MY STRENGTHS

Those who know their strengths and use them frequently tend to have more success in several areas. They feel happier, have better self-esteem, and are more likely to accomplish their goals. To use your strengths effectively, it is important to have a clear idea of what they are, and how they can be used. **Directions**: Add a checkmark to your strengths, or add your own at the bottom.

Independence ☐	Gratitude ☐	Flexibility ☐	Kindness ☐
Adventurous ☐	Logic ☐	Assertiveness ☐	Socially Aware ☐
Wisdom ☐	Discipline ☐	Athleticism ☐	Modesty ☐
Intelligence ☐	Confidence ☐	Ambition ☐	Optimistic ☐
Artistic Ability ☐	Curiosity ☐	Leadership ☐	Self Control ☐
Spirituality ☐	Common Sense ☐	Cooperation ☐	Patience ☐
Honesty ☐	Empathy ☐	Persistence ☐	Creativity ☐
Open Minded ☐	Enthusiasm ☐	Fairness ☐	Love ☐
Bravery ☐	Love of Learning ☐	Humor ☐	Forgiving ☐
Humility ☐	Teamwork ☐	Adaptability ☐	Resourceful ☐
☐	☐	☐	☐

MY STRENGTHS

Directions: Using the checklist on the previous page, answer the following prompts. Reflect on the different areas of your life.

Strengths that help you in your relationships:

1. _____
2. _____
3. _____

Strengths that help you in your profession:

1. _____
2. _____
3. _____

Strengths that help you achieve personal fulfillment:

1. _____
2. _____
3. _____

Describe a time your strengths were able to help you in your relationship:

1. _____
2. _____
3. _____

Describe a time your strengths were able to help you in your profession:

1. _____
2. _____
3. _____

Describe a time your strengths were able to help you with personal fulfillment:

1. _____
2. _____
3. _____

USING MY STRENGTHS

DAY	STRENGTH	PLAN	
Example	*Gratitude*	*I will send 3 texts to people explaining why I am grateful for them.*	☐
1			☐
2			☐
3			☐
4			☐
5			☐
6			☐
7			☐

MY STRENGTHS & QUALITIES

THINGS I AM GOOD AT...

1. _____
2. _____
3. _____

WHAT I LIKE ABOUT MY APPEARANCE...

1. _____
2. _____
3. _____

COMPLIMENTS I HAVE RECEIVED...

1. _____
2. _____
3. _____

I HAVE HELPED OTHERS BY...

1. _____
2. _____
3. _____

CHALLENGES I HAVE OVERCOME...

1. _____
2. _____
3. _____

THINGS THAT MAKE ME UNIQUE...

1. _____
2. _____
3. _____

WHAT I VALUE THE MOST...

1. _____
2. _____
3. _____

TIMES I HAVE MADE OTHERS HAPPY...

1. _____
2. _____
3. _____

HOW I GAIN ENERGY IS BY...

1. _____
2. _____
3. _____

WHAT MAKES ME CONFIDENT...

1. _____
2. _____
3. _____

I am a valuable person, just as I am!

GROWTH MINDSET

A growth mindset involves the belief that you can enhance your abilities through effort and perseverance. Conversely, a fixed mindset holds that abilities are innate and unchangeable. Embracing a growth mindset encourages you to view challenges as chances for learning and personal development.

BENEFITS

- **Build resilience.** Adopting a growth mindset helps you view challenges as a natural part of life, rather than as personal shortcomings. This perspective makes it easier to recover from difficult situations.
- **Learn from emotions.** A growth mindset encourages you to see emotions as valuable sources of insight. Instead of avoiding difficult feelings, you learn from what they reveal.
- **Strengthen relationships.** No relationship is flawless. By seeing relationships as ongoing developments, you approach relationship challenges more constructively.

EXAMPLES

SITUATION	FIXED MINDSET	GROWTH MINDSET
You are terminated from your job.	"I'm worthless. Nobody will ever hire me." *You believe your situation is permanent and things won't get better.*	"I'm upset now, but I won't feel like this forever. This is a chance to find a job I enjoy more or that pays better." *You know feelings are temporary. You find the silver linings of a difficult situation.*
Your partner decides to end the relationship.	"I am unlovable. I'll be alone forever." *You have catastrophic thinking. You believe your situation is permanent.*	"I'll allow myself time to grieve. Then, I'll reflect on the relationship and move forward." *You fully experience emotions. You reflect on what you've learned, and grow from the experience.*

I am thriving instead of surviving!

GROWTH MINDSET

TIPS FOR DEVELOPING A GROWTH MINDSET

- **Develop new skills instead of giving up.** When faced with challenges, it's tempting to quit. Instead, look for what you can learn from the situation. For instance, if you're anxious about confronting someone, see it as an opportunity to practice assertive communication
- **Face difficult situations head-on rather than avoiding them.** Challenges are a normal part of life, and not a sign of personal weakness. Confronting challenges, even if it makes you nervous, will likely show you they're more manageable than you'd imagine.
- **Look for silver linings rather than focusing on the negatives.** While life isn't perfect, there's usually a positive side to even tough situations. Consider what aspects of the challenge can help you learn and grow.
- **View challenges as temporary setbacks rather than as permanent problems.** It's easy to feel like your situation is insurmountable or won't improve, but this is often not the case. Try to see challenges as obstacles to overcome rather than permanent issues. . Ask yourself: *Will this matter to me in one month? How about in one year?*
- **Consider your emotions as sources of insight rather than avoiding them.** Rather than pushing away uncomfortable emotions, allow yourself to fully experience them. Take the time to sit with the emotion and explore what it's trying to tell you.
- **Understand the power of the word "yet".** I don't understand it...yet. I don't know how to do that...yet. I'm not good at this...yet.

What's one area in your life where you have a fixed mindset? _____

_____

_____

_____

What can you do to change your mindset so that you can grow and improve in this area?

_____

_____

_____

_____

I learn from feedback & use it to better myself!

Silver Linings

In tough times, you can choose to dwell on the negatives or seek out the positives. Studies indicate that focusing on the silver linings during challenging moments can boost your happiness and optimism. The more you practice this approach, the easier it will become to see the positive aspects. **Directions**: Complete this exercise every day for three weeks, then practice regularly for continued benefits.

Step 1: Positive Mindset
List five things that make your life enjoyable.

1. _____
2. _____
3. _____
4. _____
5. _____

Step 2: A Moment of Frustration
Briefly describe the most recent time something did not go your way, or you felt frustrated.

_____
_____
_____

Step 3: Silver Linings
Reflect on the silver linings from the step 2 situation. Describe three of the silver linings.

_____
_____
_____
_____
_____

My mistakes are opportunities for me to learn!

SELF-COMPASSION

Self-compassion is the practice of treating yourself with the same kindness, care, and understanding that you would offer to a good friend when you're facing difficulties, failures, or feelings of inadequacy.

MAIN COMPONENTS

- **Mindfulness vs. Over-Identification.** Observe your thoughts and feelings without getting caught up in them or suppressing them.
- **Self-kindness vs. Self-judgment.** Treat yourself with the same kindness and care you would offer a good friend.
- **Common Humanity vs. Isolation.** Recognize that everyone makes mistakes and experiences difficulties; you are not alone.

REFLECTIVE QUESTIONS

What would I say to a friend experiencing this? _____

_____

_____

How can I be kind to myself at this moment? _____

_____

_____

What supportive actions can I take for myself right now? _____

_____

_____

DAILY PRACTICES

- **Journaling.** Write about your feelings and offer yourself kind words.
- **Self-hug.** Wrap your arms around yourself and give a gentle squeeze.
- **Gratitude list.** Note things you are grateful for about yourself.
- **Hand on heart.** Place your hand over your heart and breathe deeply.
- **Mindful breathing.** Take a few moments each day to focus on your breath and center yourself.
- **Gentle touch.** Stroke your arm or face gently, as you might comfort a friend.

SELF-CARE CHECK-IN

Self-care activities are actions you take to support your health and enhance your well-being. Many of these activities are likely already part of your daily routine. This check-in will help you identify your self-care needs by revealing patterns and highlighting areas that might need more focus. **Directions**: Reflect on how you're performing in different aspects of self-care activities. Choose a value between 1 and 3. 1 being "poorly or rarely" and 3 being "well or often". Use the * for areas to improve.

SOCIAL SELF-CARE

1 2 3 *

- Spend time with people I like
- Have stimulating conversations
- Meet new people
- Call or write friends and family
- Spend alone time with partner

1 2 3 *

- Keep in touch with old friends
- Have intimate time with partner
- Ask others for help, when needed
- Do enjoyable activities with others
- Overall social self-care

PHYSICAL SELF-CARE

1 2 3 *

- Rest when sick
- Go to medical appointments
- Get enough sleep
- Eat regularly
- Eat healthy foods

1 2 3 *

- Take care of personal hygiene
- Exercise
- Wear clothes that make me feel good
- Participate in fun activities
- Overall physical self-care

EMOTIONAL/PSYCHOLOGICAL SELF-CARE

1 2 3 *

- Talk about my problems
- Go on vacations or day trips
- Find reasons to laugh
- Take time off from work/school
- Participate in hobbies

1 2 3 *

- Get away from distractions
- Express feelings in a healthy way
- Recognize strengths & achievements
- Do something comforting
- Overall emotional/psychological self-care

I hear myself, and understand myself!

SELF-CARE CHECK-IN

PROFESSIONAL SELF-CARE

1 2 3 *	
☐☐☐☐	Say "no" to excessive new responsibilities
☐☐☐☐	Advocate for fair pay & benefits
☐☐☐☐	Take breaks during work
☐☐☐☐	Maintain work/life balance
☐☐☐☐	Learn new things related to profession

1 2 3 *	
☐☐☐☐	Talk & build relationships with colleagues
☐☐☐☐	Improve my professional skills
☐☐☐☐	Take on projects that are interesting
☐☐☐☐	Keep a comfortable workspace
☐☐☐☐	Overall professional self-care

SPIRITUAL SELF-CARE

1 2 3 *	
☐☐☐☐	Participate in a cause
☐☐☐☐	Act in accordance with morals & values
☐☐☐☐	Set aside time for reflection
☐☐☐☐	Pray
☐☐☐☐	Spend time in nature

1 2 3 *	
☐☐☐☐	Meditate
☐☐☐☐	Recognize things that give meaning to life
☐☐☐☐	Appreciate art that is impactful
☐☐☐☐	Read a spiritual or religious book
☐☐☐☐	Overall spiritual self-care

SELF-CARE TIPS

- **Limit unhealthy self-care.** It's easy to unwind by snacking on chips and scrolling through your phone, and that's okay in moderation. However, aim to focus on healthier self-care practices.
- **Set specific self-care goals.** Rather than vague goals like "I'll make more time for self-care," try setting concrete targets such as "I'll take a 30-minute walk every evening after dinner."
- **Do things you enjoy.** Self-care is all about making time for activities that bring you joy, relaxation, or energy. Whether it's reading a book or planning a vacation, choose activities that make you feel good.
- **Allow yourself to relax.** When life gets hectic, self-care often takes a backseat. Protect your self-care time by scheduling it on your calendar or politely declining other commitments if needed.
- **Make self-care a routine.** Just as eating one apple won't make you healthy, practicing self-care only occasionally won't alleviate stress. Integrate self-care into your daily routine. For instance, make your lunchtime a break for enjoying your meal and taking a brief walk, rather than working through it.
- **Prioritize your health.** This includes eating regular meals, getting adequate sleep, exercising, and maintaining personal hygiene. While these actions may not offer immediate rewards, they contribute to long-term well-being.

I live for myself, not for anyone's expectations!

GRATITUDE EXERCISES

Gratitude involves recognizing and valuing the positive aspects of life, whether they are large or small. Incorporating gratitude into your daily routine can enhance your happiness, boost self-esteem, and offer various health benefits.

GRATITUDE LETTER
Consider someone you truly appreciate, whether they have significantly impacted your life or simply deserve a thank you. Compose a letter detailing why you value them, including specific examples and details. Decide whether you want to share the letter or keep it private.

GIVE THANKS
Throughout your day, actively look for opportunities to say "thank you." Notice when people do something positive, whether for you or others, and acknowledge their actions with a heartfelt "thank you."

GRATITUDE CONVERSATION
Engage in a dialogue with someone where you each share three things you were grateful for that day. Take time to reflect on and discuss each item, rather than rushing through the list. Make this a regular practice, perhaps before meals, at bedtime, or at another consistent time.

GRATITUDE JOURNAL
Each evening, spend a few minutes noting the positive aspects of your day. Your entries can include both significant events and simple joys, such as a satisfying meal, a pleasant conversation, or overcoming a challenge.

GRATEFUL CONTEMPLATION
Find a quiet space free from distractions like phones or TV, and spend 5-10 minutes mentally reviewing the day's positive moments. This practice can be incorporated into prayer, meditation, or done independently.

MINDFULNESS WALK
Take a walk and focus on appreciating your environment. Engage each of your senses individually: spend a moment listening, then observing your surroundings, and so on. Pay attention to details you might usually overlook, such as a gentle breeze or the texture of the clouds.

I am grateful for the little things in life that bring me joy!

SELF-ESTEEM JOURNAL

Monday		
I felt proud when...		
I felt good about myself when...		
I was proud of someone when...		

Tuesday		
Today I accomplished...		
Today was interesting because...		
Something I did for someone...		

Wednesday		
Something I did well today...		
A positive thing I witnessed...		
I had a positive experience with...		

Thursday		
Today I had fun when...		
I felt good about myself when...		
I was proud of someone when...		

Friday		
Today I accomplished...		
Today was interesting because...		
Something I did for someone...		

Saturday		
A positive thing I witnessed...		
Something I did well today...		
I had a positive experience with...		

Sunday		
I felt proud when...		
Today I had fun when...		
I felt good about myself when...		

I believe in myself more than ever before!

LETTER TO MY PAST SELF

Past regrets, losses, and traumas can have a lasting emotional impact that endures for years. In this exercise, you will revisit a past experience that still feels unresolved, write a letter to your past self, and reflect on the insights and emotions that arise. **Directions**: Recall a past experience that feels unresolved and continues to impact your life. Write the facts of the event, including your age at the time, what happened, and who was involved. Describe how this experience continues to impact your life.

_____

_____

_____

_____

_____

_____

_____

_____

_____

_____

_____

_____

_____

_____

_____

_____

_____

_____

LETTER TO MY PAST SELF

Directions: Write a letter to yourself about this unresolved experience. Address your past self with "you", be as honest as possible, and don't worry about spelling or grammar. Tell your past self any relevant insights you now have about the struggle. Offer forgiveness and compassion to your younger self. Mention anything else you feel is important to promote healing and closure.

DEAR PAST SELF,

_____
_____
_____
_____
_____
_____
_____
_____
_____
_____
_____
_____
_____
_____
_____
_____

LETTER TO MY PAST SELF

Directions: Describe any insights you had while completing the activity. Describe ways you can grow from your experience.

_____
_____
_____
_____
_____
_____
_____
_____
_____
_____
_____
_____
_____
_____
_____
_____
_____
_____
_____
_____
_____
_____

GOAL CHECKPOINT

Long-Term Goal 1

Target Date	I REACHED MY GOAL	Still Relevant?	Still Achievable?
_____	☐	☐ Yes ☐ No	☐ Yes ☐ No

How do I feel about this goal? _____

_____

_____

_____

Long-Term Goal 2

Target Date	I REACHED MY GOAL	Still Relevant?	Still Achievable?
_____	☐	☐ Yes ☐ No	☐ Yes ☐ No

How do I feel about this goal? _____

_____

_____

_____

Long-Term Goal 3

Target Date	I REACHED MY GOAL	Still Relevant?	Still Achievable?
_____	☐	☐ Yes ☐ No	☐ Yes ☐ No

How do I feel about this goal? _____

_____

_____

_____

I am open to new ways to understanding myself better!

I am here for a purpose bigger than myself!

The Purposefully Driven Boy

At last! In this section, you will focus on reflecting on your life and decide whether it aligns with your purpose and passions. You will also learn the skills needed to be the self-actualized person you were born to be.

MY VALUES

Your values represent what you consider most important in life. They guide your priorities and significantly impact your decision-making. For instance, someone who values connection might focus on nurturing their friendships, whereas someone who values wealth might prioritize their career. **Directions**: Select the 10 most important items.

Safety ☐	Achievement ☐	Fun ☐	Morals ☐
Relaxation ☐	Independence ☐	Freedom ☐	Family ☐
Creativity ☐	Justice ☐	Calmness ☐	Wealth ☐
Fairness ☐	Loyalty ☐	Variety ☐	Love ☐
Wisdom ☐	Humor ☐	Adventure ☐	Harmony ☐
Stability ☐	Honesty ☐	Free Time ☐	Pleasure ☐
Peace ☐	Responsibility ☐	Friends ☐	Status ☐
Respect ☐	Popularity ☐	Power ☐	Community ☐
Spirituality ☐	Nature ☐	Knowledge ☐	Security ☐
Beauty ☐	Recognition ☐	Success ☐	Balance ☐
☐	☐	☐	☐

MY VALUES

When a person's actions do not match their values, they may become discontent. Values are often passed down by family, and the society you live in. **Directions**: Think about the values of the people who surround you and your feelings about your own values.

MY MOTHER'S VALUES:

1. _____
2. _____
3. _____

MY FATHER'S VALUES:

1. _____
2. _____
3. _____

PERSON I RESPECT'S VALUES:

1. _____
2. _____
3. _____

SOCIETY'S VALUES:

1. _____
2. _____
3. _____

VALUES I'D LIKE TO LIVE BY:

1. _____
2. _____
3. _____

FRIENDSHIPS/SOCIAL RELATIONSHIPS

What sort of friendships would I like to have? _____
_____
_____

How can I contribute to building my ideal friendship? _____
_____
_____

WORK/CAREER/EDUCATION

What is important to me about my work, career, or education? _____
_____
_____

How would I like others to view me within my professional roles? _____
_____
_____

MY VALUES

FAMILY RELATIONSHIPS

Ideally, what would my family relationships be like?_____

_____

_____

What personal qualities would I like to contribute to my family?_____

_____

_____

MARRIAGE/INTIMATE RELATIONSHIPS

How would I describe my ideal marriage or intimate relationship?_____

_____

_____

In my ideal marriage or intimate relationship, how would I treat my partner?_____

_____

_____

SPIRITUALITY

What does "spirituality" mean to me?_____

_____

_____

In what ways is spirituality important to me?_____

_____

_____

I am capable of achieving greatness!

MY VALUES

RECREATION/RELAXATION

What are my ideal forms of recreation and relaxation? _____
_____
_____

Why are recreation and relaxation important to me? _____
_____
_____

PHYSICAL HEALTH/WELL-BEING

Ideally, how would I take care of my physical health and well-being? _____
_____
_____

Why is physical health important to me? _____
_____
_____

RECREATION/RELAXATION

How would I like to contribute to my community, or the world? _____
_____
_____

What does it mean to me to be a good member of my community, or a good citizen? _____
_____
_____

I am constantly growing and evolving!

REFLECTION POINT: MY VALUES

REFLECTION POINT: ACCOMPLISHMENTS

When we look back at our lives, it is easy to gloss over all the things that have gone well. It is natural for many of us to downplay our accomplishments, and instead focus on mistakes. In this exercise, you will be asked to look back with a focus on all the things that went right. **Directions**: Choose a timeframe to reflect on (e.g. "past year", "since starting my new job"). List your accomplishments from this timeframe. Describe a great day from this timeframe by writing what made it special. How have you grown, or what lesson did you learn? List at least three things that you are grateful for from this timeframe. What was a challenge you overcame?

TIMEFRAME

MY BEST SELF

Imagine your ideal future, what does your life look like? How would you spend your time, and who would be with you? In this exercise, envision yourself at your best, having achieved all your goals and experienced the best possible outcomes.**Directions**: On the following pages, you will imagine and describe your best possible self in three domains: personal, professional, and social. For the next week, spend 5 minutes visualizing your best possible self each day. Focus on one domain per day, cycling through each of the domains throughout the week. Record your practice in the chart below.

VISUALIZATION TIPS

- To perform visualization, picture your best possible self in as much detail as possible. Think of a scene that your best possible self might find themselves in, and imagine the sights, sounds, and feelings you would experience.
- It's common to feel distracted during visualization. If you notice your mind wandering, that's okay. Simply return your thoughts to the exercise once you become aware.

VISUALIZATION LOG

	MON.	TUES.	WED.	THUR.	FRI.	SAT.	SUN.
PERSONAL	☐	☐	☐	☐	☐	☐	☐
SOCIAL	☐	☐	☐	☐	☐	☐	☐
PROFESSIONAL	☐	☐	☐	☐	☐	☐	☐

PERSONAL DOMAIN: HOBBIES, SKILLS, PERSONALITY, ACCOMPLISHMENTS, HEALTH, ETC.

_____

_____

_____

_____

_____

_____

_____

MY BEST SELF

SOCIAL DOMAIN: FRIENDS, FAMILY, ROMANTIC RELATIONSHIPS, SOCIAL ACTIVITIES, ETC.

_____

_____

_____

_____

_____

_____

_____

_____

PROFESSIONAL DOMAIN: SKILLS, PURPOSE, JOB, EDUCATION, INCOME, RETIREMENT, ETC.

_____

_____

_____

_____

_____

_____

_____

_____

_____

REFLECTION POINT: MY BEST SELF

There's evidence that imagining our "best possible self" can help improve optimism, and motivation for change. In this exercise, you will look forward and imagine an ideal future for yourself. **Directions**: Choose a timeframe to reflect on (e.g. "next year", "during college"). What would you like to achieve during this timeframe? List at least three things you are looking forward to during this timeframe. What relationships would you like to strengthen? What can you do to help others? Give specifics about how you envision your life being different at the end of this timeframe.

TIMEFRAME

REFLECTION POINT: MY LEGACY

Channeling the wisdom of your older, wiser self offers insight into what really matters in life. **Directions**: Imagine you're reaching the end of a long, fulfilling life. Before you die, you would like to offer guidance to your present-day self. Answer the following. Looking back, what accomplishments, experiences, or realizations mattered most? How do you hope your loved ones will remember you? What advice do you want to give your younger, present-day self? Based on this advice, what goals or values are most important? What steps can your current self take to honor these goals or values?

BUILDING CREATIVITY

> Creativity is the ability to produce or develop original work, theories, techniques, or thoughts. It is a skill that can be cultivated through practice, openness, and exploration.
> **Directions**: Read each exercise, practice them on the following pages, and utilize the tips.

DAILY CREATIVITY PROMPTS
Choose one prompt each day to stimulate creative thinking. Write down your ideas, drawings, or plans based on the prompt.

MIND MAPPING
Choose a central theme, idea, or problem, and create a mind map by branching out related ideas, thoughts, and solutions. This will help you visually explore new connections and possibilities. Use the space to create your mind map with branches for ideas, sub-ideas, and connections. When you are done, identify how mind mapping helped you expand your thinking on a topic.

REVERSE THINKING
Instead of thinking about how to solve a problem, try thinking about how to make it worse or more difficult (e.g. ignore deadlines, allow distractions, etc.). Then reverse your ideas to find new creative solutions (e.g. set clear deadlines, minimize distractions, etc.).

30 CIRCLES CHALLENGE
Draw 30 circles. Try to turn as many circles as possible into something recognizable in just 5 minutes. This exercise is about speed and creativity.

"WHAT IF?"
Write three "What if?" questions that push your thinking into new, imaginative directions. Challenge yourself to think outside the box.

CREATIVE THINKING
Pick 5 describing words, and list four things that can be described using that same word.

CHANGE ONE THING
Take a well-known story, situation, or process and change one key element. Then analyze how that change would affect the outcome (e.g. If Cinderella never lost her glass slipper.).

Creativity is abundant within me!

BUILDING CREATIVITY

DAILY CREATIVITY PROMPTS

- Imagine a new invention that could solve a common problem. What would it do, and how would it work?
- Think of an everyday object. How could it be used in a completely different way?
- Create a story based on three random words. What happens in your story?
- What if you could combine two of your favorite hobbies? What would the result be?
- Design a new character for a movie, book, or comic. What are their strengths, weaknesses, and backstory?

MIND MAPPING

REVERSE THINKING

THE PROBLEM	
MAKE IT WORSE/DIFFICULT	**CREATIVE SOLUTIONS**

My imagination knows no bounds!

BUILDING CREATIVITY

30 CIRCLES CHALLENGE

"WHAT IF?"

1. _____
2. _____
3. _____

CREATIVE THINKING

1. Taste really good: _____
2. Brown: _____
3. A circle: _____
4. I don't like: _____
5. Your character: _____

CHANGE ONE THING

_____
_____
_____

My creativity empowers me!

BUILDING CREATIVITY

TIPS FOR DEVELOPING A CREATIVITY

- **Embrace curiosity.** Ask questions and explore new topics that interest you. Curiosity leads to creativity.
- **Change your environment.** Sometimes a new setting can spark fresh ideas. Try working in different locations or changing up your surroundings.
- **Challenge assumptions.** Break away from routine thinking. Challenge yourself to think differently about familiar things. Don't settle for surface-level answers.
- **Limitations foster creativity.** Give yourself constraints (e.g., create something using only three materials). Constraints force you to think creatively within limits.
- **Collaborate with others.** Engage in brainstorming sessions or creative projects with friends or colleagues. Different perspectives can inspire new ideas.
- **Try new experiences.** Experiment with new activities, hobbies, or learning opportunities. Creativity often stems from diverse experiences.
- **Play and experiment.** Allow yourself time to play, whether it's doodling, playing with materials, or trying out new ideas without worrying about the outcome.
- **Break routine.** Change your daily routine or add a new element to your day. Fresh routines stimulate creative thinking.

REFLECTION

WHAT DID YOU DISCOVER ABOUT YOUR CREATIVE POTENTIAL? WHAT NEW IDEAS OR PROJECTS WOULD YOU LIKE TO DEVELOP? WHAT STEPS CAN YOU TAKE TO CONTINUE BUILDING CREATIVITY IN YOUR LIFE?

BUILDING CURIOSITY

Curiosity is a strong desire to know or learn something. Building curiosity is a lifelong practice that opens the door to new learning, creativity, and personal growth. **Directions**: Read each exercise, practice them on the following pages, and utilize the tips.

DAILY CURIOSITY PROMPTS
Choose one prompt each day to stimulate curiosity. Write down your thoughts, questions, or insights. This will help spark curiosity and guide you toward new discoveries.

CURIOSITY-DRIVEN EXPLORATION
Take time to explore something that piques your curiosity. This could be a new book, a documentary, a podcast, or a hands-on activity (e.g. cooking, building a garden bed, etc.)

THE 5 WHYS
Choose a topic or problem you are interested in and ask "Why?" five times to dig deeper into the root of the issue. Write your responses down.

ASK BETTER QUESTIONS
Learning to ask open-ended questions can stimulate curiosity and lead to deeper understanding. Examples of good curiosity-driven questions: What makes this work the way it does? How did this idea or tradition come about? What are the consequences of this action or event? Practice writing open-ended questions about a topic of your choice.

DAILY CURIOSITY PROMPTS
- What is something you've always wondered about but never explored?
- What questions do you have about a topic you recently learned?
- What can you learn from a person whose opinions differ from yours?
- What's something you encounter every day that you've never really thought deeply about?
- What's a place you've never been but would like to know more about?

CURIOSITY-DRIVEN EXPLORATION
- What did you explore?
- What questions did it raise?
- What did you learn from this experience?
- How has it inspired you to learn more?

I enjoy the process of exploring new things!

BUILDING CURIOSITY

THE 5 WHYS

TOPIC/PROBLEM

1. Why? _____
2. Why? _____
3. Why? _____
4. Why? _____
5. Why? _____

ASK BETTER QUESTIONS

1. _____
2. _____
3. _____

TIPS FOR DEVELOPING A CURIOSITY

- **Stay open-minded.** Be willing to listen to new ideas and perspectives, even if they differ from your own.
- **Ask questions.** Whenever you encounter something unfamiliar, make it a habit to ask "Why" or "How?".
- **Read and learn.** Regularly read books, articles, or blogs on topics you know little about.
- **Observe.** Pay attention to the details around you, from nature to technology, and ask yourself what makes them function the way they do.
- **Be present.** Practice mindfulness and focus on your surroundings, allowing your natural curiosity to emerge.

REFLECTION

WHAT AREAS OF YOUR LIFE COULD BENEFIT FROM MORE CURIOSITY?

_____
_____
_____

PROBLEM SOLVING

THE PROBLEM

WHAT ARE THE CAUSES OF YOUR PROBLEM?
THINK ABOUT ALL THE POSSIBLE CAUSES. CONSIDER YOUR OWN BEHAVIOR, AS WELL AS EXTERNAL FACTORS.

DEFINE YOUR PROBLEM.
BE AS CLEAR AND COMPREHENSIVE AS POSSIBLE. DESCRIBE EACH PART OF YOUR PROBLEM.

DEVELOP MULTIPLE SOLUTIONS.
THERE ARE USUALLY MANY SOLUTIONS TO A PROBLEM, AND OUR FIRST IDEAS AREN'T ALWAYS THE BEST.

1. _____
2. _____
3. _____
4. _____
5. _____
6. _____
7. _____

I find joy in creating solutions!

PROBLEM SOLVING

ASSESS YOUR SOLUTIONS & CHOOSE ONE
YOU MIGHT COME UP WITH NEW SOLUTIONS, OR FIND THAT A COMBINATION OF SOLUTIONS MIGHT BE BETTER.

SOLUTION	STRENGTHS	WEAKNESSES

IMPLEMENT YOUR SOLUTION.
LIST SPECIFIC STEPS THAT YOU WILL TAKE TO IMPLEMENT YOUR SOLUTION.

1. _____
2. _____
3. _____
4. _____
5. _____

REVIEW.
TAKE A MOMENT TO REFLECT ON YOUR PROBLEM AND HOW YOU HANDLED IT. HOW WAS YOUR SOLUTION EFFECTIVE? IN WHAT WAYS WAS YOUR SOLUTION NOT EFFECTIVE? WHAT WOULD YOU CHANGE ABOUT HOW YOU HANDLED THE PROBLEM? WHAT ADVICE WOULD YOU GIVE TO SOMEONE DEALING WITH THE SAME PROBLEM?

_____
_____
_____
_____

BUILDING HAPPINESS

Exciting events and experiences might provide a temporary boost in happiness, but individuals usually return to their baseline level of contentment quickly. Achieving lasting joy requires effort, but you can create genuine and enduring happiness over time.

ACTS OF KINDNESS
Make a conscious effort to do something nice for no reason other than to help. You might be surprised how a simple act of kindness can turn around the day for both you and the kindness recipient.

MEDITATION
Research has linked meditation with reduced anxiety and more positive emotions. Those who meditate regularly may even permanently restructure their brains to create sustained happiness.

FOSTERING RELATIONSHIPS
Strong social connections are thought to be one of the most powerful influences on our mood. Those who are dedicated to spending time with friends and family show the highest levels of happiness. If you can't see your loved ones every day you can still send an email or make a phone call. If it feels like you never see your loved ones, schedule time that can be dedicated to them.

GRATITUDES
Write down three things you are grateful for every day. Don't worry if they seem simple or mundane, just write something down. Writing gratitudes will help you identify positive aspects of even the worst days.

EXERCISE
The positive effects of exercise are astounding. Physically active people have increased energy, superior immune systems, and a frequent sense of accomplishment. Exercise can reduce insomnia, stimulate brain growth, and even act as an antidepressant. If jogging or lifting weights seems like too much. don't be afraid to start with a 30 minute walk or a slow bike ride.

POSITIVE JOURNALING
Take some time to write positive events in your life. Write about a fund day spent with friends, a good movie, or an activity you enjoyed. Positive journaling will get you into the habit of focusing on the positive.

Happiness begins with me!

GOAL CHECKPOINT

Long-Term Goal 1

Target Date	I REACHED MY GOAL	Still Relevant?	Still Achievable?
_____	☐	☐ Yes ☐ No	☐ Yes ☐ No

Does this goal align with my values and my legacy? _____

_____

_____

_____

Long-Term Goal 2

Target Date	I REACHED MY GOAL	Still Relevant?	Still Achievable?
_____	☐	☐ Yes ☐ No	☐ Yes ☐ No

Does this goal align with my values and my legacy? _____

_____

_____

_____

Long-Term Goal 3

Target Date	I REACHED MY GOAL	Still Relevant?	Still Achievable?
_____	☐	☐ Yes ☐ No	☐ Yes ☐ No

Does this goal align with my values and my legacy? _____

_____

_____

_____

I am committed to my success!

Last Words

Congratulations on completing this workbook! By working through these exercises, you've taken important steps toward personal growth, self-awareness, and developing new skills. It was designed to help you reflect, challenge yourself, and unlock your potential. By reaching this point, you've already made significant progress.

But remember, growth is a lifelong journey. While this workbook may come to an end, the lessons and insights you've gained are just the beginning. Continue to apply what you've learned, stay curious, and remain committed to becoming the best version of yourself.

Whenever you face challenges, remember that the tools and strategies you've explored here are always available to you. Return to these pages when you need inspiration, and trust in your ability to overcome obstacles and embrace new opportunities. Life will continue to challenge you, but with the mindset and skills you've developed, you are prepared to navigate it with resilience and confidence.

Thank you for taking this journey. May it inspire you to continue growing, learning, and living a life filled with purpose, passion, and fulfillment. The path ahead is yours to create!

Follow us on Instagram and Facebook @gbadulting to join the community of Girls & Boys Adulting.

You have come so far, celebrate yourself because you deserve it!

Acknowledgements

Putting this workbook together has been an exciting and challenging experience. I am deeply grateful to my "community" who brought *A Life Changing Workbook for Boys Adulting* to life. I really could not have done this without you guys.

To my mother, Rosalin Clovis, for obvious reasons that just need to be written down. I literally would not be here if it was not for her. Witnessing her overcome obstacles and continuously building her resilience, has given me a blueprint for how to be adaptable and flexible in my life. A lot of what I have learned does not come from a fancy school (heavy on the fancy... shoutout to SPELMAN COLLEGE), but from just observing my mother live her life. As an adult, my mother is my best friend and keeps me on my toes. She constantly helps me think outside of the box. Even though she complains about me asking a million and one questions (something she thought I would grow out of), I am glad I have her in my corner. She motivates me every day to strive to be the best version of myself. I would not be where I am today without her love and support. I LOVE YOU MOMMY!!!

To my first roommate, my sister, Monique Montgomery (heavy on the Monique Montgomery...iykyk), for always challenging me and giving me different perspectives. She has always been there to support me, so I made it a goal of mine to be the sister to her that she is to me. The bar is high though.

It's amazing when your board members are friends. This is for [Dr.] Shanta', Andrienne, and Joshua Bent, for the help and encouragement provided in executing my vision. I would not have been able to complete this workbook without the daily check-ins, much needed breaks, and love.

For every teacher, professor, manager, dean, counselor, who believed in me even though I could not see the vision at the time, THANK YOU! I see the vision now, and it is so clear. As one of my favorite professors said to me after graduation, "just be who you're supposed be". That stuck with me, and will forever be how I live my life.

And finally to my clients who have trusted me with their personal growth and constantly inspire me to find ways to change the world, one life at a time.

My heart is so full!

Made in the USA
Columbia, SC
12 November 2024

45621709R00083